Computer words you gotta know!

Computer words you gotta know!

Essential definitions for survival in a high-tech world

Alan Freedman

Author of the award-winning *The Computer Glossary*

amacom
American Management Association

New York • Atlanta • Boston • Chicago • Kansas City • San Francisco • Washington, D.C.
Brussels • Toronto • Mexico City

This book is available at a special discount when ordered in bulk quantities. For information, contact Special Sales Department, AMACOM, a division of American Management Association, 135 West 50th St., New York, NY 10020.

This publication is designed to provide accurate and authoritative information in regard to the subject matter covered. It is sold with the understanding that the publisher is not engaged in rendering legal, accounting, or other professional service. If legal advice or other expert assistance is required, the services of a competent professional person should be sought.

Library of Congress Cataloging-in-Publication Data

Freedman, Alan, 1942-
    Computer words you gotta know! : essential definitions for survival
in a high-tech world / Alan Freedman.
        p.   cm.
    ISBN 0-8144-7814-X
    1. Computers--Dictionaries.   2. Electronic data processing-
-Dictionaries.   I. Title.
QA76.15.F7345   1993
004'.03--dc20   93-12235
                                                                       CIP

© 1993 The Computer Language Company Inc.
All rights reserved.
Printed in the United States of America.

Printing number

10   9   8   7   6   5   4   3   2   1

To Irmalee

ILLUSTRATIONS: Irma Lee Morrison, Eric Jon Nones, Joseph D. Russo
EDITORIAL/PRODUCTION: Irma Lee Morrison
COPY EDITING: Mary McCann
TYPESET BY: The Computer Language Company Inc., Point Pleasant, PA 18950
PRINTER: HP LaserJet III with LaserMaster WinJet board (800 dpi)

CONTENTS

A NOTE FROM THE AUTHOR

If you're involved in our high-tech world today, it helps to understand basic computer terminology. If you have a personal computer or are involved with information systems in your organization, it may be downright necessary.

This book contains over 2,000 terms, excerpted and abbreviated from the sixth edition of *The Computer Glossary* and Version 6.1 of *Electronic Computer Glossary*, which contains nearly 6,000 terms. I've tried to include the most widely-known hardware and software products as well as general computer jargon and concepts. If a term is not in this book, it's probably in *Electronic Computer Glossary*, which is updated quarterly. New terms are coined every day in this industry.

If you're new to computers, be sure to look up the terms in the *WORDS YOU GOTTA KNOW* list located in the front of this book.

Good luck and good fortune.

ACKNOWLEDGMENTS

I'd like to acknowledge all the people who have helped me in this endeavor, which really started in 1981 with the first edition of *The Computer Glossary*. I've called on hundreds of vendors for information and countless colleagues for consultation and advice. Thank you, all of you, who have willingly contributed.

There are always those who just keep on helping, and I'd especially like to thank Pam Brannan, Steve Diascro, Thom Drewke, Max Fetzer, Jim Farrell, Lynn Frankel, Steve Gibson, Pete Hermsen, Joel Orr, Mark and Joan Shapiro, Jim Stroh, Skip Vaccarello, Dave Wallace, Irv Wieselman and Paul and Jan Witte.

HOW SYSTEMS RELATE

The following diagram depicts the interrelationships of systems within the computer industry from a manager's point of view.

The management system is the set of goals, objectives, strategies, tactics, plans and controls within an organization. The information system is the database and application programs that turn the raw data into information required by management. The computer system is the machinery that automates the process. Understanding this relationship has helped thousands of non-technical people make sense out of this field.

This perspective is contained in the definitions in this book.

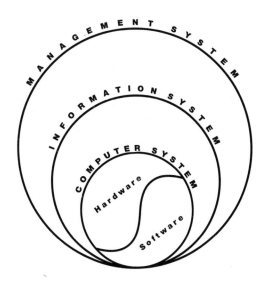

WORDS YOU REALLY GOTTA KNOW!

COMPUTER SYSTEM FUNDAMENTALS
hardware
software
data
information
computer
personal computer
computer system
bit
byte
memory
peripheral
hard disk
floppy disk
printer
monitor
modem
mouse
bus
operating system
LAN
analog
digital
scanner
CD ROM

PERSONAL COMPUTERS
PC
Macintosh
DOS
Windows
menu
icon
function keys
DBMS
spreadsheet
business graphics
word processing
text editor
paint program
drawing program
GUI
multimedia
communications program
x86

INFORMATION SYSTEM FUNDAMENTALS
information system
prototyping
system development cycle
batch processing
transaction processing
master file
transaction file

USE ACRONYMS!

Most of the terms in this book are referenced by their acronyms. For example, you won't find OPEN SYSTEMS INTERCONNECT in the book, but you will find OSI. The reason for this is that 99% of the time you hear a term by its acronym, not its full name. Eliminating full titles also saves lines of paper and allows more definitions to be printed in the allotted space of this book.

IF YOU CAN'T FIND A TERM...

LOOK UP ITS ACRONYM!

A/D converter (**A**nalog to **D**igital **C**onverter) Device that converts analog signals from instruments that monitor such conditions as movement, temperature, sound, etc., into binary code for the computer. See *modem*, *codec* and *D/A converter*.

abend (**AB**normal **END**) Also called a *crash* or *bomb*, occurs when the computer is presented with instructions or data it cannot recognize or the program is reaching beyond its protective boundary. It is the result of erroneous software logic or hardware failure.

abort (1) To exit a function or application without saving any data that has been changed.

(2) To stop a transmission.

accelerator board Add-in board that replaces the existing CPU with a higher performance CPU. See *graphics accelerator*.

acceptance test Test performed by the end user to determine if the system is working according to the specifications in the contract.

access To store data on and retrieve data from a disk or other peripheral device. See *access arm* and *access method*.

access arm Mechanical arm that moves the read/write head across the surface of a disk similar to a tone arm on a phonograph.

access charge Charge imposed by a communications service or telephone company for the use of its network.

access code (1) Identification number and/or password used to gain access into a computer system.

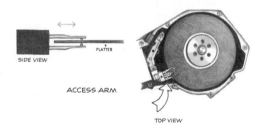

(2) Number used as a prefix to a calling number in order to gain access to a particular telephone service.

access method Software routine that is part of the operating system or network control program which performs the storing/retrieving or transmitting/receiving of data. It is also responsible for detecting a bad transfer of data caused by hardware or network malfunction and correcting it if possible.

access time Measurement of the speed of memory (RAM chips) or disk drives.

acoustic coupler Device that connects a terminal or computer to the handset of a telephone. It contains a shaped foam bed that the handset is placed in, and it may also contain the modem.

active matrix LCD LCD technology that uses a transistor behind each pixel. It provides a sharp, bright display and eliminates submarining. Color active matrix screens use a transistor for each red, green and blue dot. Contrast with *passive matrix LCD*.

address (1) Number of a particular memory or peripheral storage location. Like post office boxes, each byte of memory and each disk sector has its own unique address.

(2) As a verb, to manage or work with. For example, "the computer can address 2MB of memory."

address space Total amount of memory that can be used by a program. It may refer to a physical limit or to a virtual limit; for example, the 386 can address 4GB of physical memory and 64TB of virtual memory.

Adobe Type Manager PostScript font utility for the Macintosh and Windows from Adobe Systems, Inc., Mountain View, CA. It scales Type 1 fonts into screen fonts and prints them on non-PostScript dot matrix and HP laser printers. See *PostScript*.

agent Software routine that waits in the background and performs an action when a specified event occurs. For example, it could alert the user when a certain transaction has arrived.

AI (**A**rtificial **I**ntelligence) Devices and applications that exhibit human intelligence and behavior including robots, expert systems, voice recognition, natural and foreign language processing. It also implies the ability to learn or adapt through experience.

Note: The term intelligence refers to processing capability; therefore, every computer is intelligent. But, artificial intelligence implies human-like intelligence. An ironic twist in terminology.

algorithm Set of ordered steps for solving a problem, such as a mathematical formula or the instructions in a program.

alias (1) Alternate name used for identification, such as for naming a field or a file.

(2) Phony signal created under certain conditions when digitizing voice.

aliasing In computer graphics, the stair-stepped appearance of diagonal lines. See *anti-aliasing*.

alpha test First test of newly developed hardware or software in a laboratory setting. The next step is *beta testing* with actual users.

alphanumeric Use of alphabetic letters mixed with numbers and special characters as in name, address, city and state. The text you're reading is alphanumeric.

ALU (**A**rithmetic **L**ogic **U**nit) High-speed circuit in the CPU that does the actual calculating and comparing.

AM (**A**mplitude **M**odulation) Transmission technique that blends the data into a carrier by varying the amplitude of the carrier. See *modulate*.

analog Representation of an object that resembles the original. Analog devices monitor conditions, such as movement, temperature and sound, and convert them into analogous electronic or mechanical patterns. For example, an analog watch represents the planet's rotation with the rotating hands on the watch face. Telephones turn voice vibrations into electrical vibrations of the same shape. Analog implies continuous operation in contrast with digital, which is broken up into numbers.

AND, OR & NOT Fundamental operations of Boolean logic. See *Boolean search*.

anomaly Abnormality or deviation. It is a favorite word among computer people when complex systems produce output that is inexplicable.

ANSI See *standards bodies*.

ANSI character set ANSI character set that defines 256 characters. The first 128 are standard ASCII, and the second 128 contain math and foreign language symbols, which are different than those on the PC. See *extended ASCII*.

anti-aliasing In computer graphics, a category of techniques that is used to smooth the jagged appearance of diagonal lines. For example, the pixels that surround the edges of the line are filled in with varying shades of gray or color in order to blend the sharp edge into the background. See *dithering*.

antivirus Program that detects and removes a virus.

API (**A**pplication **P**rogram **I**nterface) Language and message format used by a program to activate and interact with functions in another program or in the hardware. See *interface*.

app Same as *application*.

APPC See *LU 6.2*.

Apple See *vendors*.

Apple II Personal computer family from Apple that helped pioneer the microcomputer revolution. It has been widely used in schools and home. The Apple IIe is the only model that is still made.

APPLE IIe

AppleTalk Apple's local area network protocol. It supports Apple's proprietary LocalTalk access method as well as Ethernet and Token Ring. AppleTalk and LocalTalk are built into all Macs, IIGS's and LaserWriters.

application (1) Specific use of the computer, such as payroll, inventory and billing. (2) Same as application program and software package.

application developer Individual that develops a business application and usually performs the duties of a systems analyst and application programmer.

application development language Same as *programming language*.

application development system Programming language and associated utility programs that allow for the creation, development and running of application programs. A DBMS, including query languages and report writers, may be included.

application generator Software that generates application programs from descriptions of the problem rather than by traditional programming. It is one or more levels higher than a high-level programming language.

application program Any data entry, update, query or report program that processes data for the user.

application programmer Individual who writes application programs in a user organization. Most programmers are application programmers. Contrast with *systems programmer*.

APPN (**A**dvanced **P**eer-to-**P**eer **N**etworking) Routing and other enhancements in IBM's SNA network that allow for improved performance and administration in a distributed computing environment.

archive (1) To copy data onto a different disk or tape for backup. Archived files are often compressed to maximize storage media.

(2) To save data onto the disk.

archive attribute File classification that indicates the file has not been backed up. It is used by various copy and backup programs.

ARCNET (**A**ttached **R**esource **C**omputer **NET**work) First local area network technology. It provides an economical alternative to Token Ring and Ethernet.

argument In programming, a value passed between programs, subroutines or functions. Arguments are independent items, or variables, that contain data or codes. See *parameter*.

array Ordered arrangement of data elements. A vector is a one dimensional array, a matrix is a two-dimensional array.

array processor Computer, or extension to its arithmetic unit, that is capable of performing simultaneous computations on elements of an array of data in some number of dimensions. See *vector processor* and *math coprocessor*.

artificial intelligence See *AI*.

artificial language Language that has been predefined before it is ever used. Contrast with *natural language*.

AS/400 (**A**pplication **S**ystem/400) IBM minicomputer series introduced in 1988 that supersedes and advances the System/36 and System/38.

ASCII (**A**merican **S**tandard **C**ode for **I**nformation **I**nterchange) Pronounced "ask-ee." A binary code for data that is used in communications, most minicomputers and all personal computers. Only the first 128 characters (0-127) within the 256 combinations in a byte conform to the ASCII standard. The rest are used differently depending on the computer.

ASCII file Data or text file that contains characters coded in ASCII. Text files, batch files and source language programs are usually ASCII files. ASCII files are used as a common denominator between incompatible formats, since most applications can export and import ASCII files. Contrast with *binary file*.

ASCII protocol Simplest form of transmitting ASCII data. It implies little or no error checking.

ASCII sort Sequential order of ASCII data. In ASCII code, lower case characters follow upper case. True ASCII order would put the words DATA, data and SYSTEM into the following sequence:

DATA SYSTEM   data

aspect ratio Ratio of width to height of an object.

assembler Software that translates assembly language into machine language. Contrast with *compiler*, which is used to translate a high-level language, such as COBOL or C, into assembly language first and then into machine language.

assembly language Programming language that is one step away from machine language. Each assembly language statement is translated into one machine instruction by the assembler. There is a different assembly language for each CPU series.

Although often used synonomously, assembly language and machine language are not the same. Assembly language is turned into machine language. For example, the assembly instruction COMPARE A,B is translated into COMPARE contents of memory bytes 2340-2350 with 4567-4577 (where A and B happen to be located). The physical binary format of the machine instruction is specific to the computer it's running in.

asymmetric multiprocessing Multiprocessing design in which each CPU is dedicated to a specific function. Contrast with *symmetric multiprocessing*.

asymmetric system (1) System in which major components or properties are different.

(2) In video compression, a system that requires more equipment to compress the data than to decompress it.

asynchronous transmission
Transmission of data in which each character is a self-contained unit with its own start and stop bits. Intervals between characters may be uneven. It is the common method of transmission between a computer and a modem, although the modem may switch to synchronous transmission to communicate with the other modem. Also called start/stop transmission.

Common asynchronous protocols are Kermit, Xmodem, Ymodem and Zmodem. Contrast with *synchronous transmission*.

AT (**A**dvanced **T**echnology) IBM's first 286-based PC, introduced in 1984. It was the most advanced machine in the PC line and featured a new keyboard, 1.2MB floppy and 16-bit data bus. AT-class machines run considerably faster than XTs (8088-based PCs). See *PC*.

AT bus Refers to the 16-bit bus introduced with the AT. It was an extension of the 8-bit XT bus. Also called ISA bus. See *XT bus* and *EISA*. Contrast with *Micro Channel*.

IBM AT

AT class Refers to PCs that use the 286 CPU and the 16-bit AT (ISA) bus.

AT command set Series of machine instructions used to activate features on an intelligent modem. Developed by Hayes Microcomputer Products, Inc., it is used by most every modem manufacturer. AT is a mnemonic code for ATtention, the prefix that initiates each command. See *Hayes Smartmodem*.

AT interface See *AT bus*.

ATM (1) (**A**utomatic **T**eller **M**achine) Special-purpose banking terminal that allows users to make deposits and withdrawals.

(2) (**A**synchronous **T**ransfer **M**ode) High-speed packet switching technique suitable for MANs and broadband ISDN transmission.

(3) See *Adobe Type Manager*.

attribute (1) In relational database management, a field within a record.

(2) For printers and display screens, a characteristic that changes a font, for example, from normal to boldface or from normal to underlined.

(3) See *file attribute*.

audio Range of frequencies within human hearing (approx. 20Hz at the low to a high of 20,000Hz).

audio board Same as *sound card*.

audio response See *voice response*.

audiotex Voice response application that allows users to enter and retrieve information over the telephone in response to a voice menu. It is used for obtaining the latest financial quotes as well as for ordering products.

audiovisual Audio and/or video capability.

audit Examination of systems, programming and datacenter procedures in order to determine the efficiency of computer operations.

audit software Specialized programs that perform a variety of audit functions, such as sampling databases and generating confirmation letters to customers. It can highlight exceptions to categories of data and alert the examiner to possible error.

audit trail Record of transactions in an information system that provides verification of the activity of the system. The simplest audit trail is the transaction itself. If a person's salary is increased, the change transaction includes the date, amount of raise and name of authorizing manager.

authoring program Software that allows for the development of tutorials and CBT programs.

authorization code Identification number or password that is used to gain access to a local or remote computer system.

auto (**AUTO**matic) Refers to a wide variety of devices that perform unattended operation.

auto answer Modem feature that accepts a telephone call and establishes the connection. See *auto dial.*

auto dial Modem feature that opens the line and dials the telephone number of another computer to establish connection. See *auto answer.*

auto resume Feature that lets you stop working on the computer and take up where you left off at a later date without having to reload applications. Memory contents are stored on disk or kept active by battery and/or AC power.

AutoCAD Full-featured CAD program from AutoDesk Inc., Sausalito, CA, that runs on PCs, VAXs, Macs and UNIX workstations. Originally developed for CP/M machines, it was one of the first major CAD programs for personal computers and became an industry standard.

AUTOEXEC.BAT (**AUTO**matic **EXEC**ute **BAT**ch) File of DOS commands that is automatically executed upon startup. It is easily modified by the user.

automation
Replacement of manual operations by computerized methods. Office automation refers to integrating clerical tasks such as typing, filing and appointment scheduling. Factory automation refers to computer-driven assembly lines.

autosave Saving data to the disk at periodic intervals without user intervention.

autosizing Ability of a monitor to maintain the same rectangular image size when changing from one resolution to another.

autostart routine
Instructions built into the computer and activated when it is turned on. The routine performs diagnostics and then loads the operating system and passes control to it.

autotrace Routine that locates outlines of raster graphics images and converts them into vector graphics.

A VISION OF AUTOMATION (Circa 1890)
(Courtesy Rosemont Engineering)

B

b-spline In computer graphics, a curve that is generated using a mathematical formula which assures continuity with other b-splines.

back up To make a copy of important data onto a different storage medium for safety.

backbone In communications, the part of a network that handles the major traffic. It may interconnect multiple locations, and smaller networks may be attached to it.

background (1) Non-interactive processing in the computer. See *foreground/background*.

(2) Base, or backdrop, color on screen.

background processing Processing in which the program is not visibly interacting with the user. With an advanced multitasking operating system, background programs may be given any priority from low to high. In a non-multitasking environment, background tasks are run when foreground tasks are idle, such as between keystrokes.

backlit LCD screen that has its own light source from the back of the screen, making the background brighter and characters appear sharper.

backplane (1) Reverse side of a panel or board that contains interconnecting wires.

(2) Printed circuit board, or device, containing slots, or sockets, for plugging in boards or cables.

backup Additional resources or duplicate copies of data on different storage media for emergency purposes.

backup & recovery Combination of manual and machine procedures that can restore lost data in the event of hardware or software failure. Routine backup of databases and system logs that keep track of the computer's operations are part of a backup & recovery program.

backup copy Disk, tape or other machine readable copy of a data or program file. Making backup copies is a discipline that most computer users learn the hard way-- after a week's work is lost.

backup disk Disk that is used to hold duplicate copies of important files. High-density floppy disks and removable disks cartridges are used for backup disks.

backup power Additional power source that can be used in the event of power failure. See *UPS*.

backup tape See *tape backup*.

backward compatible Same as *downward compatible*.

bad sector Segment of disk storage that cannot be read or written due to a physical problem in the disk. Bad sectors on hard disks are marked by the operating system and bypassed. If data is recorded in a sector that becomes bad, data recovery software, and sometimes special hardware, must be used to restore it.

band (1) Range of frequencies used for transmitting a signal. A band is identified by its lower and upper limits; for example, a 10MHz band in the 100 to 110MHz range.

(2) Contiguous group of tracks that are treated as a unit.

bandwidth Transmission capacity of a computer channel, communications line or bus. It is expressed in cycles per second (Hertz), the bandwidth being the difference between the lowest and highest frequencies transmitted. The frequency is equal to or greater than the bits per second. Bandwidth is also often stated in bits or bytes per second.

bank Arrangement of identical hardware components.

bank switching Engaging and disengaging electronic circuits. Bank switching is used when the design of a system prohibits all circuits from being addressed or activated at the same time requiring that one unit be turned on while the others are turned off.

bar chart Graphical representation of information in the form of bars. See *business graphics*.

bar code Printed code used for recognition by a scanner. Traditional one-dimensional bar codes use the bar's width as the code, but encode just an ID or account number. Two-dimensional systems, such as PDF 417 from Symbol Technology, hold 1,800 characters in an area the size of a postage stamp. See *UPC*.

base (1) Starting point or reference point.

(2) Component in a bipolar transistor that activates the switch. Same as *gate* in a MOS transistor.

(3) Multiplier in a numbering system. In a decimal system, each digit position is worth 10x the position to its right. In binary, each digit position is worth 2x the position to its right.

baseband Communications technique in which digital signals are placed onto the transmission line without change in modulation. Common baseband LAN techniques are token passing ring (Token Ring) and CSMA/CD (Ethernet).

In baseband, the full bandwidth of the channel is used, and simultaneous transmission of multiple sets of data is accomplished by interleaving pulses (TDM). Contrast with *broadband* transmission, which transmits data, voice and video simultaneously by modulating each signal onto a different frequency (FDM).

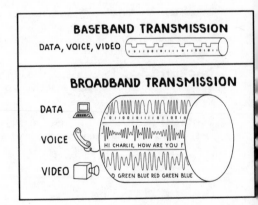

BASEBAND TRANSMISSION
DATA, VOICE, VIDEO

BROADBAND TRANSMISSION
DATA
VOICE   HI CHARLIE, HOW ARE YOU F
VIDEO   GREEN BLUE RED GREEN BLUE

BASIC See *programming languages.*

BAT file (**BAT**ch file) File of DOS or OS/2 commands, which are executed one after the other. It has a .BAT extension and is created with a text editor or word processor. See *AUTOEXEC.BAT.*

batch Group, or collection, of items.

batch data entry Entering a group of source documents into the computer.

batch file (1) File containing data that is processed or transmitted from beginning to end.

(2) File containing instructions that are executed one after the other. See *BAT file.*

batch file transfer Consecutive transmission of two or more files.

batch job Same as *batch program.*

batch operation Some action performed on a group of items at one time.

batch processing Processing a group of transactions at one time. Transactions are collected and processed against the master files (master files updated) at the end of the day or some other time period. Contrast with *transaction processing.*

Batch and Transaction Processing

Information systems typically use both batch and transaction processing methods. For example, in an order processing system, transaction processing is the continuous updating of the customer and inventory files as orders are entered.

At the end of the day, batch processing programs generate picking lists for the warehouse. At the end of the week or some other period, batch programs print invoices and management reports.

batch program Non-interactive (non-conversational) program such as a report listing or sort.

batch session Transmitting or updating an entire file. Implies a non-interactive or non-interruptible operation from beginning to end. Contrast with *interactive session.*

batch total Sum of a particular field in a collection of items that is used as a control total to ensure that all data has been entered into the computer. For example, using account number as a batch total, all account numbers would be summed manually before entry into the computer. After entry, the total is checked with the computer's sum of the numbers. If it does not match, source documents are manually checked against the computer's listing.

baud (1) Signalling rate of a line. It's the switching speed, or number of transitions (voltage or frequency changes) that are made per second. Only at low speeds are bauds equal to bits per second; for example, 300 baud is equal to 300 bps. However, one baud can be made to represent more than one bit per second. For example, the V.22bis modem generates 1200 bps at 600 baud.

(2) Commonly (and erroneously) used to specify bits per second for modem speed; for example, 1200 baud means 1200 bps. See previous paragraph.

baud rate Redundant reference to baud. Baud is a rate.

baudot code Pronounced "baw-doh." One of the first standards for international telegraphy developed in the late 19th century by Emile Baudot. It uses five bits to make up a character.

BBS (**B**ulletin **B**oard **S**ystem) Computer system used as an information source and message system for a particular interest group. Users dial into the BBS, review and leave messages for other users as well as conference with current users on the system. BBSs are used to distribute shareware and may provide access (doors) to application programs.

BCD (**B**inary **C**oded **D**ecimal) Storage of numbers in which each decimal digit is converted into binary and is stored in a single character or byte. For example, a 12-digit number would take 12 bytes. Contrast with *binary number*.

benchmark Test of performance of a computer or peripheral device.

Bernoulli Box Removable disk system for personal computers from Iomega Corp., Roy, UT. The name comes from 18th century Swiss scientist, Daniel Bernoulli, who demonstrated fluid dynamics principles. Unlike a hard disk in which the read/write head flies over a rigid disk, the Bernoulli floppy is spun at high speed and bends up close to the head. Upon power failure, a hard disk must retract the head to prevent a crash, whereas the Bernoulli floppy naturally bends down.

beta test Test of hardware or software that is performed by users under normal operating conditions. See *alpha test*.

Bezier In computer graphics, a curve that is generated using a mathematical formula which assures continuity with other Bezier curves. It is mathematically simpler, but more difficult to blend than a b-spline curve.

binary Meaning two. The fundamental principle behind digital computers. All input to the computer is converted into binary numbers made up of the two digits 0 and 1 (bits). For example, when you press the "A" key on your personal computer, the keyboard generates and transmits the number 01000001 to the computer's memory as a series of pulses. The 1 bits are transmitted as high voltage; the 0 bits are transmitted as low. The bits are stored as a series of charged and uncharged memory cells in the computer and as positively and negatively charged spots on tape and disk. Display screens and printers convert the binary numbers into visual characters.

binary code Coding system made up of binary digits. See *BCD* and *data code*.

binary compatible Refers to any data, hardware or software structure (data file, machine code, instruction set, etc.) in binary form that is 100% identical to another.

binary field Field that contains binary numbers. It may refer to the storage of binary numbers for calculation purposes, or to a field that is capable of holding any information, including data, text, graphics images, voice and video.

binary file (1) Program in machine language form ready to run.

(2) File that contains binary numbers.

binary format (1) Numbers stored in pure binary form in contrast with *BCD* form. See *binary numbers*.

(2) Any machine-readable information.

(3) File transfer mode that transmits any type of file without loss of data.

binary notation Use of binary numbers to represent values.

binary numbers Numbers stored in pure binary form. Within one byte (8 bits), the values 0 to 255 can be held. Two contiguous bytes (16 bits) can hold values from 0 to 65,535. Contrast with *BCD*.

binary search Technique for quickly locating an item in a sequential list. The desired key is compared to the data in the middle of the list. The half that contains the data is then compared in the middle, and so on, either until the key is located or a small enough group is isolated to be sequentially searched.

bionic Machine that is patterned after principles found in humans or nature; for example, robots. It also refers to artificial devices implanted into humans replacing or extending normal human functions.

BIOS (**B**asic **I/O S**ystem) Detailed instructions that activate peripheral devices. See *ROM BIOS*.

bit (**BI**nary digi**T**) Single digit in a binary number (0 or 1). In the computer, a bit is physically a transistor in a memory cell, a magnetic spot on disk or tape or a high or low voltage pulsing through a circuit.

Groups of bits make up storage units in the computer, called bytes and words, which are manipulated as a group. Bytes always contain eight bits and hold one alphanumeric character. Words refer to the computer's internal registers and processing capacity (8-bit, 16-bit, 32-bit, 64-bit), the larger the number, the more data the computer processes at one time. See *space/time*.

OFF
"0"

ON
"1"

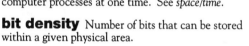
BIT

bit density Number of bits that can be stored within a given physical area.

bit depth Number of on-screen colors (number of bits used to represent a pixel).

bitblt (**BIT BL**ock **T**ransfer) In graphics accelerators and graphics engines, a hardware feature that moves a rectangular block of bits from main memory into video memory. It speeds the display of moving objects (animation, scrolling) on screen.

bite See *byte*.

bitmap (1) In computer graphics, an area in memory that represents the video image. For monochrome screens, one bit in the bitmap represents one pixel on screen. For gray scale or color, several bits in the bitmap represent one pixel or group of pixels on screen.

(2) Binary representation in which each bit or set of bits corresponds to some object (image, font, etc.) or condition.

bitmapped font Set of dot patterns for each letter and digit in a particular typeface. Each font size requires a different set of dot patterns. Contrast with *scalable font*.

bitmapped graphics Raster graphics method for generating images. Contrast with *vector graphics* and *character graphics*.

black box Custom-made electronic device, such as a protocol converter or encryption system. Yesterday's black boxes often become today's off-the-shelf products.

blank character Space character that takes up one byte in the computer just like a letter or digit. When you press the space bar on a personal computer keyboard, the ASCII character with the numeric value of 32 is created.

blank squash Removal of blanks between items of data. For example, in the expression **CITY + ", " + STATE**, the data is concatenated with a blank squash resulting in AUSTIN, TX rather than AUSTIN   TX.

block (1) Group of disk or tape records that is stored and transferred as a single unit.

(2) Group of bits or characters that is transmitted as a unit.

(3) Group of text characters that has been marked for moving, copying, saving or other operation.

block diagram Chart that contains squares and rectangles connected with arrows to depict hardware and software interconnections. For program flow charts, information system flow charts, circuit diagrams and communications networks, more elaborate graphical representations are usually used.

board See *printed circuit board* and *BBS*.

boilerplate Common phrase or expression used over and over. Boilerplate is stored on disk and copied into the document as needed.

boldface Characters that are heavier and darker on printed output and brighter than normal on a display screen.

Boolean logic The "mathematics of logic," developed by the English mathematician George Boole in the mid 19th century. Its rules and operations govern logical functions (true/false) rather than numbers. As add, subtract, multiply and divide are the primary operations of arithmetic, AND, OR and NOT are the primary operations of Boolean logic.

Boolean search Search for specific data. It implies that any condition can be searched for using the Boolean operators AND, OR and NOT. For example, the English language request: "Search for all the Spanish and French speaking employees who have MBAs, but don't work in Sales." is expressed in the dBASE command language as follows:

```
list for degree = "MBA" .and.
   (language = "Spanish" .or. language = "French")
    .and. .not. department = "Sales"
```

boot Causing the computer to start executing instructions. Personal computers contain built-in instructions in a ROM chip that are automatically executed on startup. These instructions search for the operating system, load it and pass control to it. Starting up a large computer may require more button pushing and keyboard input.

The term comes from "bootstrap," since bootstraps help you get your boots on, booting the computer helps it get its first instructions. See *cold boot* and *warm boot*.

boot drive Disk drive that contains the operating system.

boot failure Inability to locate and/or read the operating system from the designated disk.

boot ROM Memory chip that allows a workstation to be booted from the server or other remote station.

boot sector Area on disk (usually the first sectors in the first disk partition) reserved for the operating system. On startup, the computer looks in the boot sectors for the operating system.

bootable disk Disk that contains the operating system and typically refers to a floppy disk. If a hard disk personal computer does not find a bootable floppy disk in the primary floppy drive at startup, it boots from the hard disk.

bootstrap See *boot*.

Borland See *vendors*.

Boston Computer Society, The World's largest personal computer association, founded in 1977 by Jonathan Rotenberg. Services include user and special interest groups, subscription to BCS publications, access to the Resource Center, public domain software and shareware. Address is One Kendall Square, Cambridge, MA 02139.

bpi (**B**its **P**er **I**nch) Used to measure the number of bits stored in a linear inch of a track on a recording surface, such as on a disk or tape.

bps (**B**its **P**er **S**econd) Used to measure the speed of data transfer in a communications system.

break To temporarily or permanently stop executing, printing or transmitting.

break key Key that is pressed to stop the execution of the current program or transmission.

breakout box Device inserted into a multiple-line cable for testing purposes that provides an external connecting point to each wire. A small LED may be attached to each line, which glows when a signal is present.

bridge (1) To cross from one circuit, channel or element over to another.

(2) Device that connects two networks of the same type together. See *gateway* and *router*.

broadband Technique for transmitting large amounts of data, voice and video over long distances. Using high frequency transmission over coaxial cable or optical fibers, broadband transmission requires modems for connecting terminals and computers to the network. Using the same technique as cable TV, several streams of data can be transmitted simultaneously. Contrast with and see *baseband* for illustration.

browse To view and possibly edit a file of data on screen similar to handling text in a word processing document. The user can scroll the data horizontally and vertically.

bubble memory Solid state semiconductor and magnetic storage device suited for rugged applications. It is about as fast as a slow hard disk and holds its content without power.

buffer Reserved segment of memory used to hold data while it is being processed. In a program, buffers are created to hold some amount of data from each of the files that will be read or written. A buffer may also be a small memory bank used for special purposes.

buffer flush Transfer of data from memory to disk.

bug Persistent error in software or hardware. If the bug is in software, it can be corrected by changing the program. If the bug is in hardware, new circuits have to be designed. The term was coined in the 1940s when a moth was found squashed between the points of an electromechanical relay in the Mark I. Contrast with *glitch*.

A Note from the Author

On October 19, 1992, I found my first "real bug." When I fired up my laser printer, it printed blotchy pages. Upon inspection, I found a bug lying belly up in the trough below the charging wire. The printer worked fine after removing it!

bundled/unbundled Complete package of hardware and software for a single price. *Unbundled* systems have separate prices for each component.

bunny suit Protective clothing worn by an individual in a clean room that keeps human bacteria from infecting the chip-making process. The outfit makes people look like oversized rabbits.

burn in To test a new electronic system by running it for some length of time. Weak components often fail within the first few hours of use.

burst mode Alternate method of high-speed transmission in a communications or computer channel. Under certain conditions, the system can send a burst of data at higher speed for some period of time. For example, a multiplexor channel may suspend tranmission of several streams of data and send one high-speed transmission using the entire bandwidth.

BUNNY SUIT
(Coutesy Hewlett-Packard Company)

bus Common pathway between hardware devices. A computer bus connects the CPU with its main memory and to the memory banks that reside on the control units of the peripheral devices. It is made up of two parts. Addresses are sent over the address bus to signal a memory location and the data is transferred over the data bus to that location.

   A network bus is a common cable that interconnects all stations in the network. Signals are broadcast to all nodes at once, and the requested station responds.

bus extender (1) Board that pushes a printed circuit board out of the way of surrounding boards for testing purposes. It plugs into an expansion slot, and the expansion board plugs into the bus extender.

(2) Device that extends the length of a bus.

(3) Device that increases the number of expansion slots. It is either an expansion board containing multiple expansion slots, or an expansion board that cables to a separate housing that contains the slots and its own power supply.

bus mastering Bus design that allows add-in boards to process independently of the CPU and to be able to access the computer's memory and peripherals on their own.

bus mouse Mouse that plugs into an expansion board. It takes up an expansion slot whereas a serial mouse takes up a

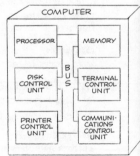

COMPUTER BUS

serial port. The choice depends on how many devices must be connected to each type of socket.

business analyst Individual who analyzes the operations of a department or functional unit with the purpose of developing a general systems solution to the problem that may or may not require automation. The business analyst can provide insights into an operation for an information systems analyst.

business graphics Numeric data represented in graphic form. While line graphs, bar charts and pie charts are the common forms of business graphics, there are many additional graphic representations available.

business machine

Any office machine, such as a typewriter or calculator, that is used in clerical and accounting functions. The term has traditionally excluded computers and terminals.

  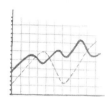

PIE CHART   BAR CHART   GRAPH

button Physical button on a device, such as a mouse, or a simulated button on screen that is "pushed" by moving the cursor onto it and clicking the mouse.

byte Common unit of computer storage from micro to mainframe. It is made up of eight binary digits (bits). A ninth bit may be added as a parity bit for error checking.

A byte holds the equivalent of a single character, such as the letter A, a dollar sign or decimal point. For numbers, a byte can hold a single decimal digit (0 to 9), two numeric digits (packed decimal) or a number from 0 to 255 (binary numbers).

C

C, C++ See *programming languages*.

C2 Minimum security level defined by the National Computer Security Center.

CA (**C**omputer **A**ssociates) See *vendors*.

cache Pronounced "cash." A reserved section of memory used to improve performance.

A disk cache is a reserved section of normal memory or additional memory on the disk controller board. When the disk is read, a large block of data is copied into the cache. If subsequent requests for data can be satisfied in the cache, a slower disk access is not required. If the cache is used for writing, data is queued up in memory and written to the disk in larger blocks.

A memory cache is a high-speed memory bank between memory and the CPU. Blocks of instructions and data are copied into the cache and instruction execution and data updating are performed in the higher-speed memory.

CASH MEMORY EXAMPLES

caching controller Disk controller with a built-in cache. See *cache*.

CAD (**C**omputer-**A**ided **D**esign) Using computers to design products. CAD systems are high-speed workstations or personal computers using CAD software and input devices such as graphic tablets and scanners. CAD output is a printed design or electronic input to CAM systems (see *CAD/CAM*).

CAD/CAM (**C**omputer-**A**ided **D**esign/**C**omputer-**A**ided **M**anufacturing) Integration of CAD and CAM. Products designed by CAD are direct input into the CAM system. For example, a device is designed and its electronic image is translated into a numerical control programming language, which generates the instructions for the machine that makes it.

CAE (**C**omputer-**A**ided **E**ngineering) Software that analyzes designs which have been created in the computer or that have been created elsewhere and entered into the computer. Different kinds of engineering analyses can be performed, such as structural analysis and electronic circuit analysis.

CAI (**C**omputer-**A**ssisted **I**nstruction) Same as CBT.

CAL (**C**omputer-**A**ssisted **L**earning) Same as CBT.

calculated field Numeric or date field that derives its data from the calculation of other fields. Data is not entered into a calculated field by the user.

CAM (**C**omputer-**A**ided **M**anufacturing) Automated manufacturing systems and techniques, including numerical control, process control, robotics and materials requirements planning (MRP). See CAD/CAM.

canned program Software package that provides a fixed solution to a problem. Canned business applications should be analyzed carefully as they usually cannot be changed much, if at all.

canned routine Program subroutine that performs a specific processing task.

card See *printed circuit board, magnetic stripe, punched card* and *HyperCard*.

card reader Peripheral device that reads magnetic stripes on the back of a credit card.

caret Up-arrow (^) symbol used to represent a decimal point or the control key. For example, **^Y** means Ctrl-Y. It is the shift-6 key on the keyboard.

carpal tunnel syndrome Compression of the main nerve to the hand due to scarring or swelling of the surrounding soft tissue in the wrist (area formed by carpal bones on top and muscle tendons below). Caused by trauma, arthritis and improper positioning of the wrist, it can result in severe damage to the hands.

carriage Printer or typewriter mechanism that holds the platen and controls paper feeding and movement.

carriage return See *return key*.

carrier Alternating current that vibrates at a fixed frequency, used to establish a boundary, or envelope, in which a signal is transmitted. Carriers are commonly used in radio transmission (AM, FM, TV, microwave, satellite, etc.) in order to differentiate transmitting stations. For example, an FM station's channel number is actually its carrier frequency. The FM station merges (modulates) its audio broadcast (data signal) onto its carrier and transmits the combined signal over the airwaves. At the receiving end, the FM tuner latches onto the carrier frequency, filters out the audio signal, amplifies it and sends it to the speaker.

carrier frequency Unique frequency used to "carry" data within its boundaries. It is measured in cycles per second, or Hertz.

cartridge Self-contained, removable storage module that contains disks, magnetic tape or memory chips. Cartridges are inserted into slots in the drive, printer or computer.

TAPE CARTRIDGE

CASE (**C**omputer **A**ided **S**oftware **E**ngineering or **C**omputer **A**ided **S**ystems **E**ngineering) Software used in any and all phases of developing an information system, including analysis, design and programming. The ultimate goal of

CASE is to provide a language for describing the overall system that is sufficient to generate all the necessary programs.

case sensitive Distinguishing lower case from upper case. In a case sensitive language, "abc" is considered different data than "ABC."

cash memory See *cache*.

cassette Removable storage module that contains a supply reel of magnetic tape and a takeup reel. Data cassettes look like audio cassettes, but are made to higher tolerances.

TAPE CASSETTE

CBT (**C**omputer-**B**ased **T**raining) Using the computer for training and instruction. CBT programs are called *courseware* and provide interactive training sessions for all disciplines.

CCITT See *standards bodies*.

CCP (**C**ertificate in **C**omputer **P**rogramming) Award for successful completion of an examination in computer programming. See *CDP*.

CD (**C**ompact **D**isc) Audio disc that contains up to 72 minutes of hi-fi stereo sound. CDs are recorded in digital form as a series of microscopic pits (binary code) covered with a clear, protective plastic layer. A laser shines onto the pits and the reflections are decoded.

CD caddy Plastic container that holds a CD ROM disc. The caddy is inserted into the disc drive.

CD-I (**C**ompact **D**isc-**I**nteractive) Compact disc format that holds data, audio, still video and animated graphics. It provides up to 144 minutes of CD-quality stereo, up to 9.5 hours of AM-radio-quality stereo or up to 19 hours of monophonic audio.

CD ROM (**C**ompact **D**isc **R**ead **O**nly **M**emory) Compact disc format used to hold text, graphics and hi-fi stereo sound. It's like a music CD, but uses a different track format for data. The music CD player cannot play CD ROMs, but CD ROM players usually play music CDs and have output jacks for headphones or amplified speakers.

CD ROMs hold in excess of 600MB of data, which is equivalent to about 250,000 pages of text or 20,000 medium-resolution images.

CD ROM Extensions Software required to use a CD ROM player on a PC running DOS. It usually comes with the player and includes a driver specialized for the player as well as Microsoft's MSCDEX.EXE driver.

CDP (**C**ertificate in **D**ata **P**rocessing) Award for the successful completion of an examination in hardware, software, systems analysis, programming, management and accounting. Institute for Certification of Computer Professionals, Des Plaines, IL.

central processing unit See *CPU*.

central processor Same as *CPU*.

centralized processing Processing performed in one or more computers in a single location. All terminals throughout the organization are connected to the computers in the datacenter. Contrast with *distributed processing* and *decentralized processing.*

Centronics Common parallel port standard used in personal computers. Centronics Corp. was the maker of the first commercially successful dot matrix printer.

CGA (**C**olor/**G**raphics **A**dapter) IBM video display standard that provides low-resolution text and graphics. It has been superseded by EGA and VGA.

CGM (**C**omputer **G**raphics **M**etafile) Standard format for interchanging graphics images.

channel Pathway between components in a computer system or between workstations in a network.

character Single alphabetic letter, numeric digit, or special symbol such as a decimal point or comma. A character is equivalent to a byte; for example, 50,000 characters take up 50,000 bytes.

character cell Matrix of dots used to form a single character on a display screen or printer. For example, an 8x16 character cell is made up of 16 horizontal rows each containing eight dots.

character code Same as *data code.*

character graphics Set of symbols strung together like letters of the alphabet to create graphics. DOS applications on the PC often create forms and rulers using single-line and double-line character graphics.

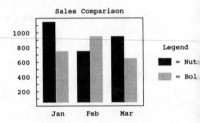

CHARACTER GRAPHICS

check bits Calculated number used for error checking. The number is derived by some formula from the binary value of one or more bytes of data. See *parity checking, checksum* and CRC.

check box Small box that displays an X or checkmark when the associated option is selected.

check digit Numeric digit used to ensure that account numbers are correctly entered into the computer. Using a formula, a check digit is calculated for each new account number, which then becomes part of the number, often the last digit.
    When an account number is entered, the data entry program recalculates the check digit and compares it to the check digit entered. If the digits are not equal, the account number is considered invalid.

checksum Value used to ensure data is transmitted without error. It is created by adding the binary value of each alphanumeric character in a block of data and sending it with the data. At the receiving end, a new checksum is computed and matched against the transmitted checksum. A non-match indicates an error.

chicklet keyboard Keyboard with small, square keys not suitable for touch typing.

child In database management, the data that is dependent on its parent. See *parent-child*.

child program Secondary or subprogram called for and loaded into memory by the main program. See *parent program*.

chip Integrated circuit. Chips are squares or rectangles that measure approximately from 1/16th to 5/8th of an inch on a side. They are about 1/30th of an inch thick, although only the top 1/1000th of an inch holds the actual circuits. Chips contain from a few dozen to several million electronic components (transistors, resistors, etc.). The terms *chip*, *integrated circuit* and *microelectronic* are synonymous.

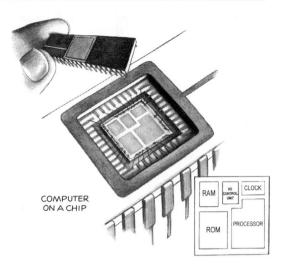

COMPUTER ON A CHIP

RAM   I/O CONTROL UNIT   CLOCK

ROM   PROCESSOR

CICS (**C**ustomer **I**nformation **C**ontrol **S**ystem) Software from IBM that provides transaction processing for its mainframes. It is called a TP monitor and it controls the interaction between users and their applications and also lets programmers develop screen displays without detailed knowledge of the terminals used.

CIM (**C**omputer-**I**ntegrated **M**anufacturing) Integrating office/accounting functions with automated factory systems. Point of sale, billing, machine tool scheduling and supply ordering are part of CIM.

CIO (**C**hief **I**nformation **O**fficer) Executive officer in charge of all information processing in an organization.

ciphertext Data that has been coded (enciphered, encrypted, encoded) for security purposes.

circuit (1) Set of electronic components that perform a particular function in an electronic system.

(2) Same as *communications channel*.

circuit analyzer Device that tests the validity of an electronic circuit.

circuit board Same as *printed circuit board*.

circuit switching Temporary connection of two or more communications channels. Users have full use of the circuit until the connection is terminated. Contrast with *message switching*, which stores messages and forwards them later, and contrast with *packet switching*, which breaks up a message into packets and routes each packet through the most expedient path at that moment.

CISC (**C**omplex **I**nstruction **S**et **C**omputer) Pronounced "sisk." Traditional computer architecture that executes very comprehensive instructions. Contrast with *RISC*.

class In object-oriented programming, a user-defined data type that defines a collection of objects that share the same characteristics.

clean room Room in which the air is highly filtered in order to keep out impurities.

clear memory To reset all RAM and hardware registers to a zero or blank condition. Rebooting the computer may or may not clear memory, but turning the computer off and on again guarantees that memory is cleared.

click To select an object by pressing the mouse button when the cursor is pointing to the required menu option or icon.

client Workstation or personal computer in a client/server environment.

client/server Architecture in which the client is the requesting machine (personal computer or workstation) and the server is the supplying machine (LAN file server, mini or mainframe). The client provides the user interface and performs some or most of the application processing. The server maintains the databases and processes requests from the client to extract data from or update the database. The server also controls the application's integrity and security. Contrast with *centralized processing*, in which dumb (non-processing) terminals are connected to a mini or mainframe.

clip art Set of canned images used to illustrate word processing and desktop publishing documents.

clipboard Reserved memory used to hold data that has been copied from one application in order to be inserted into another.

Clipper Application development system for PCs from Computer Associates. Originally a dBASE compiler, it become a stand-alone development system with many features. It was developed by Nantucket Corporation, later acquired by CA.

clipping level Disk's ability to maintain its magnetic properties and hold its content. A high-quality level range is 65-70%; low quality is below 55%.

clock Internal timing device. The CPU clock is the computer's heartbeat. It uses a quartz crystal to generate a uniform electrical frequency.
   A realtime clock is a time-of-day clock that keeps track of hours, minutes and seconds.

clock/calendar Internal time clock and month/year calendar that is kept active with a battery.

clock doubling Doubling the internal processing speed of a CPU while maintaining the original clock speed for I/O (transfers in/out of the chip). Intel popularized the technique with its Speed Doubler chips.

clock speed Internal speed of a computer. For example, the same CPU running at 20MHz is twice as fast internally as one running at 10MHz.

clone Device that works like the original, but does not necessarily look like it. It implies 100% functional compatibility.

closed With regard to a switch, closed is "on." Open is "off."

closed architecture System whose technical specifications are not made public. Contrast with *open architecture*.

closed system System in which specficiations are kept proprietary to prevent third-party hardware or software from being used. Contrast with *open system*.

cluster Some number of disk sectors (typically 2 to 16) treated as a unit. The entire disk is divided into clusters, each one a minimum increment of storage. Thus, a 30-byte file may use up 2,048 bytes on disk if the disk cluster is four 512-byte sectors.

CMOS (**C**omplementary **MOS**) Pronounced "C moss." Type of integrated circuit widely used for processors and memories.

CMOS RAM (1) Memory made of CMOS chips.

(2) Small, battery-backed memory bank in a personal computer used to hold time, date and system information such as drive types.

CMYK (**C**yan **M**agenta **Y**ellow blac**K**) Color model used for printing. In theory, cyan, magenta and yellow (CMY) can print all colors, but inks are not pure and black comes out muddy. Black ink is required for quality printing.

co-resident Program or module that resides in memory along with other programs.

coaxial cable High-capacity cable used in communications and video, commonly called co-ax. It contains an insulated solid or stranded wire surrounded by a solid or braided metallic shield, which is wrapped in an external cover.

COBOL See *programming languages*.

code (1) Set of machine symbols that represents data or instructions. See *data code* and *machine language*.

(2) Any representation of one set of data for another. For example, a parts code. product type or discount code.

COAXIAL CABLE

(3) To write a program. See *source code* and *line of code*.

(4) To encode for security purposes. See *encryption*.

code generator See *application generator* and *macro recorder*.

code page In DOS 3.3 and higher, a table that sets up the keyboard and display characters for various foreign languages.

codec (**CO**der-**DEC**oder) Electronic circuit that converts voice or video into digital code (and vice versa) using techniques such as pulse code modulation and delta modulation. A codec is an A/D and D/A converter.

coder (1) Junior, or trainee, programmer who writes simple programs or writes the code for a larger program that has been designed by someone else.

(2) Person who assigns special codes to data.

cold boot Starting the computer by turning power on. Turning power off and then back on again clears memory and many internal settings. Some program failures will lock up the computer and require a cold boot to use the computer again. In other cases, only a warm boot is required. See *warm boot* and *boot*.

cold start Same as *cold boot*.

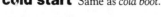

collating sequence Sequence, or order, of the character set built into a computer.

color printer Printer that prints in color using dot matrix, electrophotographic, Cycolor, electrostatic, ink jet or thermal-transfer techniques.

color separation Separating a picture by colors in order to make negatives and plates for color printing. Full color requires four separations, cyan, magenta, yellow and black (CMYK).

COM (**C**omputer **O**utput **M**icrofilm) Creating microfilm or microfiche from computer output. A COM machine can be online or stand-alone (transfer via tape/disk).

COM file (**COM**mand file) Executable DOS or OS/2 program that takes up less than 64K and uses a .COM file extension. See *EXE file*.

COM port Serial communications port on a PC. See COM1 and *serial port*.

COM1 Logical name assigned to serial port #1 in DOS and OS/2. COM ports are usually connected to a modem or mouse and sometimes to a printer. DOS versions up to 3.2 support COM1 and COM2. Version 3.3 supports up to COM4, and OS/2 supports eight COM ports. Contrast with *LPT1*.

comma delimited Record layout that separates data fields with a comma and usually surrounds character data with quotes, for example:

```
"Pat Smith","5 Main St.","New Hope","PA","18950"
"K. Jones","34 E. 88 Ave.","Syosset","NY","10024"
```

command (1) Order given to the computer by the user. See *command-driven* and *menu-driven*.

(2) Programming language directive. Contrast with *function*.

command-driven Program that accepts commands as typed-in phrases. It is usually harder to learn, but may offer more flexibility than a menu-driven program. Once learned, command-driven programs may be faster to use, because the user can state a request succinctly. Contrast with *menu-driven*.

command interpreter Same as *command processor*.

command language Special-purpose language that accepts a limited number of commands, such as a query language, job control language (JCL) or command processor. Contrast with *programming language*, which is a general purpose language.

command line In a command-driven system, the area on screen that accepts typed-in commands.

command mode Operating mode that causes the computer or modem to accept commands for execution.

command processor Software that accepts a limited number of user commands and converts them into low-level commands required by the operating system or some other control program or application.

COMMAND.COM Command processor for DOS and OS/2. COMMAND.COM accepts your typed-in commands and executes them.

comment Descriptive statement in a source language program that is used for documentation.

commercial software Software that is designed and developed for sale to the general public.

communications Electronic transfer of information from one location to another. *Data communications* refers to digital transmission, and *telecommunications* refers to all forms of transmission, including digital and analog voice and video. See *communications protocol.*

communications channel Also called a *circuit* or *line*, it is a pathway over which data is transferred between remote devices. It may refer to the physical medium (telephone line, optical fiber, coaxial cable or twisted wire pair), or it may refer to one of several carrier frequencies transmitted simultaneously within the same line.

communications program Software that manages the transmission of data between computers and terminals. In personal computers, it manages transmission to and from the computer's serial port. It includes several communications protocols and can usually emulate dumb terminals for hookup to minis and mainframes.

In a file server, the communications program is called the *network operating system*, (NetWare, LANtastic, etc.). In mini and mainframe networks, the programs that support communications are called *access methods*, *network control programs* and TP *monitors*. See *front end processor.*

communications protocol Hardware and software standards that govern transmission between two stations. On personal computers, communications programs offer a variety of protocols (Kermit, Xmodem, Zmodem, etc.) to transfer files via modem. On LANs, protocols are embodied in Ethernet, Token Ring and other access methods. In mainframe networks, there are multiple levels of protocols, and protocols within protocols. It's a complicated business managing enterprise-wide networks. See *OSI* and *SNA.*

The following conceptual exchange is at the data link level (Zmodem, Ethernet, etc.), which ensures that a block of data is transferred between two nodes without error.

The Data Link Protocol

Are you there? **Yes, I am.** Are you ready to receive? **Yes, I am.** Here comes the message--bla, bla, bla-- did you get it? **Yes, I did.** Here comes the next part--bla, bla, bla-- did you get it? **No, I didn't.** Here it comes again-- bla, bla, bla-- did you get it? **Yes, I did.** There is no more. Goodbye. **Goodbye.**

communications satellite Radio relay station in orbit 22,300 miles above the equator. It travels at the same rate of speed as the earth (geosynchronous), so it appears stationary.

Compaq See *vendors.*

compare Fundamental computer capability. By comparing one set of data with another, the computer can locate, analyze, select, reorder and make decisions. After comparing, the computer can indicate whether the data were equal or which set was numerically greater or less than the other.

compilation Compiling a program. See *compiler*.

compiler (1) Software that translates a high-level programming language (COBOL, C, etc.) into machine language. A compiler usually generates assembly language first and then translates the assembly language into machine language.

(2) Software that converts a high-level language into a lower-level representation. For example, a help compiler converts a text document embedded with appropriate commands into an online help system. A dictionary compiler converts terms and definitions into a dictionary lookup system.

complement Number derived by subtracting a number from a base number. For example, the tens complement of 8 is 2. Complements are used in digital circuits, because it's faster to subtract by adding complements than by performing true subtraction.

component One element of a larger system. A hardware component can be a device as small as a transistor or as large as a disk drive as long as it is part of a larger system. Software components are routines or modules within a larger system.

composite video Video-only (no audio) part of a TV signal. Early personal computers used composite video output for TV hookup.

compound document Text file that contains both text and graphics. Eventually it will routinely hold voice annotations and video clips. See *OLE*.

compression See *data compression*.

compression ratio Measurement of compressed data. For example, a file compressed into 1/4th of its original size can be expressed as 4:1, 25%, 75% or 2 bits per byte.

CompuServe See *online services*.

compute To perform mathematical operations or general computer processing.

compute bound Same as *process bound*.

computer General-purpose machine that processes data according to a set of instructions that are stored internally either temporarily or permanently. The computer and all the equipment attached to it are called *hardware*. The instructions that tell it what to do are called *software*. A set of instructions that perform a particular task is called a program, or *software program*.

computer architecture Design of a computer system. It sets the standard for all devices that connect to it and all the software that runs on it. It is based on the type of programs that will run (business, scientific, etc.) and the number of them that must be run concurrently.

Computer Associates See *vendors*.

computer designer Person who designs the electronic structure of a computer.

computer exchange Commodity exchange through which the public can buy and sell used computers. After a match, the buyer sends a check to the exchange and the seller sends the equipment to the buyer. If the buyer accepts it, the money is sent to the seller minus a commission. For information, contact the following exchanges:

BOSTON COMPUTER EXCHANGE, 617/542-4414, FAX 617/542-8849
NATIONAL COMPUTER EXCHANGE, 212/614-0700, FAX 212/777-1290
THE NEWMAN GROUP, 313/426-3200, FAX 313/426-0777

computer graphics See *graphics*.

computer language Programming language, machine language or the language of the computer industry.

computer on a chip Single chip that contains the processor, RAM, ROM, clock and I/O control unit. It is used for myriads of applications from automobiles to toys.

computer power Effective performance of a computer. It can be expressed in MIPS (millions of instructions per second), clock speed (10MHz, 16MHz) and in word or bus size, (16-bit, 32-bit). However, as with automobile horsepower, valves and cylinders, such specifications are only guidelines. The real power of a computer system is net throughput, which is how long it takes to get the job done.

A software package is "powerful" if it has a large number of features.

computer science Field of computer hardware and software. It includes systems analysis & design, application and system software design and programming and datacenter operations. Contrast with *information science*.

computer system
Complete computer made up of the CPU, memory and related electronics (main cabinet), all the peripheral devices connected to it and its operating system.
Computer systems fall into ranges called *microcomputers* (personal computers), *minicomputers* and *mainframes*, roughly small, medium and large.

COMSAT (**COM**munications **SAT**ellite Corp.) Private company that provides services to AT&T, MCI and others. In 1965, it launched Early Bird, the first commercial satellite.

concatenate To link structures together.
Concatenating files appends one file to another. In speech synthesis, units of speech called phonemes (k, sh, ch, etc.) are concatenated to produce meaningful sounds.

concentrator Device that joins several communications channels together. It is similar to a

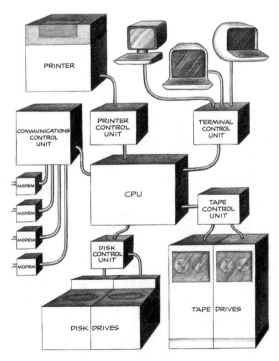

COMPUTER SYSTEM

multiplexor, except that it does not spread the signals back out again on the other end. The receiving computer performs that function.

conditioning Extra cost options in a private telephone line that improve performance by reducing distortion and amplifying weak signals.

CONFIG.SYS DOS and OS/2 configuration file. It resides in the root directory and is used to load drivers and change settings at startup.

configuration Makeup of a system. To configure a system is to choose from a variety of options in order to create a customized environment.

configuration file File that contains information about a specific user, program, computer or file.

connect time Amount of time a user at a terminal is logged on to a computer system. See *online services* and *service bureau*.

connectivity Communications between computers.

connector (1) Any plug, socket or wire that links two devices together.

(2) In database management, a link or pointer between two data structures.

(3) In flowcharting, a symbol that is used to break a sequence and resume the sequence elsewhere. It is often a small circle with a number or other identification written in it.

console (1) Main operator's terminal on a large computer.

(2) Any display terminal.

consultant Independent specialist. Consultants can act as advisors, or they can perform detailed systems analysis & design functions. They can help users formulate their information requirements and produce a generalized or detailed set of specifications from which hardware or software vendors can respond. Consultants are often used as project advisors throughout the entire system development cycle.

contention resolution Process of resolving which device gains access to a resource when both are in contention.

context sensitive help Help screens that provide specific information about the condition or mode the program is in at the time help is sought.

context switching (1) In a multitasking environment, to turn control over to another program under direction of the operating system. A program's context is its current state.

(2) To stop working in an application and go work in another under direction of the user.

contextual search To search for records or documents based upon the text contained in any part of the file as opposed to searching on a pre-defined key field.

contiguous Adjacent or touching. Contrast with *fragmentation*.

control code One or more characters used to control a device, such as a display screen or printer. Control codes often begin with an escape character (ASCII 27); however, this is only one example. There is an endless number of codes used to control electronic devices.

Control Data See *vendors*.

control key Abbreviated "ctrl" or "ctl." Key that is pressed with a letter or digit key to command the computer; for example, holding down control and pressing U, turns on underline mode in many word processors. The caret (shift-6) also represents the control key: ^Y means control-Y.

control program Software that controls the operation of and has highest priority in a computer. Operating systems, network operating systems and network control programs are examples. Contrast with *application program*.

control unit (1) Within the processor, the circuitry that locates, analyzes and executes each instruction in the program.

(2) Within the computer, a *control unit*, or *controller*, is hardware that controls peripheral activities such as a disk or display screen. Upon signals from the CPU, it performs the physical data transfers between memory and the peripheral device.

Personal computer control units are contained on a single printed circuit board. In large computers, control units are on one or more printed circuit boards, or they may be housed in a stand-alone cabinet.

In single chip computers, a built-in control unit accepts keyboard input and provides serial output to a display.

conventional memory In a PC, the first megabyte of memory. The term may also refer only to the first 640K. The top 384K of the first megabyte is called *high DOS memory* or *upper memory area (UMA)*.

conventional programming Using a procedural language.

conversion (1) Data conversion is changing data from one file or database format to another. It may also require code conversion between ASCII and EBCDIC.

(2) Media conversion is changing storage media such as from tape to disk.

(3) Program conversion is changing the programming source language from one dialect to another, or changing application programs to link to a new operating system or DBMS.

(4) Computer system conversion is changing the computer model and peripheral devices.

(5) Information system conversion requires data conversion and either program conversion or the installation of newly purchased or created application programs.

converter (1) Device that changes one set of codes, modes, sequences or frequencies to a different set. See *A/D converter*.

(2) Device that changes current from 60Hz to 50Hz, and vice versa.

cooperative processing Sharing a job among two or more computers such as a mainframe and a personal computer. It implies splitting the workload for the most efficiency.

coordinate Belonging to a system of indexing by two or more terms. For example, points on a plane, cells in a spreadsheet and bits in dynamic RAM chips are identified by a pair of coordinates. Points in space are identified by sets of three coordinates.

coprocessor Secondary processor used to speed up operations by handling some of the workload of the main CPU. See *math coprocessor*.

copy To make a duplicate of the original. In digital electronics, all copies are identical.

copy buster Program that bypasses the copy protection scheme in a software program and allows normal, unprotected copies to be made.

copy protection Resistance to unauthorized copying of software. Copy protection was never an issue with mainframes and minicomputers, since vendor support has always been vital in those environments.

In the early days of floppy-based personal computers, many copy protection methods were used. However, with each scheme introduced, a copy buster program was developed to get around it. When hard disks became the norm, copy protection was abolished. In order to manage a hard disk, files must be easily copied.

core Round magnetic doughnut that represents one bit in a core storage system. A computer's main memory used to be referred to as core or core storage.

Corel Draw Popular windows-based illustration program for 286 and higher PCs from Corel Systems Corp., Ottawa, Ontario. Introduced in 1989, it includes over 100 fonts and is known for its speed and ease of use. It generates its own CDR vector graphics files, but can import other graphics formats.

cost/benefits analysis Study that projects the costs and benefits of a new information system. Costs include people and machine resources for development as well as running the system.

counter Hardware device or software routine that keeps track of some function.

courseware Educational software. See CBT.

CP/M (Control Program for Microprocessors) Single user operating system for the 8080 and Z80 microprocessors from Digital Research. Created by Gary Kildall, CP/M pioneered the microcomputer revolution in business and had its heyday in the early 1980s.

CPM (Critical Path Method) Project management planning and control technique implemented on computers. The critical path is the series of activities and tasks in the project that have no built-in slack time. Any task in the critical path that takes longer than expected will lengthen the total time of the project.

cpi (1) (Characters Per Inch) Measures the density of characters per inch on tape or paper. A printer's CPI button switches character pitch.

(2) (Counts Per Inch) Measures the resolution of a mouse/trackball as flywheel notches per inch (horizontal and vertical flywheels rotate as the ball is moved). Notches are converted to cursor movement.

cps (Characters Per Second) Measures the speed of a serial printer or the speed of a data transfer between hardware devices or over a communications channel. CPS is equivalent to bytes per second.

CPU (Central Processing Unit) Also called the *processor*, it is the computing part, or "brains" of the computer and is made up of the control unit and the ALU. It obtains its instructions and data from memory and contains the circuits that perform mathematical (add, subtract, etc.) and logical operations (compare) on the data.

The CPU, clock and main memory make up a computer. A complete computer system requires the addition of control units, input, output and storage devices and an operating system.

CPU bound Same as *process bound*.

CPU chip Same as *microprocessor*.

CPU time Amount of time it takes for the CPU to execute a set of instructions and explicitly excludes the waiting time for input and output.

CR (**C**arriage **R**eturn) Return key on a keyboard or the actual code that is generated when the key is pressed (decimal 13, hex 0D).

CR/LF (**C**arriage **R**eturn/**L**ine **F**eed) End of line characters used in standard PC text files (ASCII 13 10). In the Mac, only the CR is used; in UNIX, the LF.

crash See *abend* and *head crash*.

Cray See *vendors*.

CRC (**C**yclical **R**edundancy **C**hecking) Error checking technique used to ensure the accuracy of transmitting digital code over a communications channel. The transmitted messages are divided into predetermined lengths which, used as dividends, are divided by a fixed divisor. The remainder of the calculation is appended onto and sent with the message. At the receiving end, the computer recalculates the remainder. If it does not match the transmitted remainder, an error is detected.

cross tabulate To analyze and summarize data. For example, cross tabulation is used to summarize the details in a database file into totals in a spreadsheet.

crossfoot Numerical error checking technique that compares the sum of the columns with the sum of the rows.

crosshatch Criss-crossed pattern used to fill in sections of a drawing to distinguish them from each other.

crosstalk (1) In communications, an interference from an adjacent channel.

(2) (Crosstalk) Family of PC communications programs from DCA/Crosstalk Communications, Alpharetta, GA.

CRT (**C**athode **R**ay **T**ube) Vacuum tube used as a display screen in a video terminal or TV. The term often refers to the entire terminal.

crunch (1) To process data as in "number crunching."

(2) To compress data. See *data compression*.

cryogenics Using materials that operate at very cold temperatures. See *superconductor*.

cryptography Same as *encryption*.

crystal See *quartz crystal*.

CSMA/CD (**C**arrier **S**ense **M**ultiple **A**ccess/**C**ollision **D**etection) Communications access method. When a device wants to gain access to the network, it checks to see if the network is free. If it is not, it waits a random amount of time before retrying. If the network is free and two devices attempt access at exactly the same time, they both back off to avoid a collision and each wait a random amount of time before retrying.

Ctl, Ctrl See *control key*.

CTO (**C**hief **T**echnical **O**fficer) Executive responsible for overall technical direction.

current directory Disk directory the system is presently working in. Unless otherwise specified, commands that deal with disk files imply the current directory.

cursor (1) Movable symbol on screen that is the contact point between the user and the data. In text systems, the cursor is a blinking rectangle or underline. and it is moved by the mouse or the Home, End, PgUp, PgDn and four Arrow keys. On graphic systems, it is also called a pointer, and it can take any shape (arrow, square, paintbrush, etc.), which changes as it is moved into different parts of the screen.

(2) Pen-like or puck-like device used with a graphics tablet. As the tablet cursor is moved across the tablet, the screen cursor moves correspondingly. See *mouse*.

customized software Software designed for an individual customer.

cut & paste To move a block of text from one part of a document to another or from one file to another.

cyberpunk Relating to futuristic delinquency: hackers breaking into computer banks, survival based on high-tech wits. Stems from science fiction novels such as "Neuromancer" and "Shockwave Rider."

cyberspace Term coined by William Gibson in his novel "Neuromancer," to refer to a futuristic computer network that people use by plugging their brains into it! See *virtual reality.*

cycle (1) Single event that is repeated. For example, in a carrier frequency, one cycle is one complete wave.

(2) Set of events that is repeated. For example, in a polling system, all of the attached terminals are tested in one cycle.

cycle stealing CPU design technique that periodically "grabs" machine cycles from the main processor usually by some peripheral control unit, such as a DMA (direct memory access) device. In this way, processing and peripheral operations can be performed concurrently or with some degree of overlap.

cycle time Time interval between the start of one cycle and the start of the next cycle.

cycles per second Number of times an event or set of events is repeated in a second. See *Hertz.*

cylinder Aggregate of all tracks that reside in the same location on every disk surface. On multiple-platter disks, the cylinder is the sum total of every track with the same track number on every surface. On a floppy disk, a cylinder comprises the top and corresponding bottom track.

When storing data, the operating system fills an entire cylinder before moving to the next one. The access arm remains stationary until all the tracks in the cylinder have been read or written.

D

D/A converter (**D**igital to **A**nalog **C**onverter) Device that converts digital pulses into analog signals. See *A/D converter*.

D&B Software See *vendors*.

daemon Pronounced "demon." Program that waits in the background ready to perform some action when a certain event occurs. From Greek mythology meaning "guardian spirit." Same as *agent*.

daisy chain Arrangement of devices connected in series, one after the other. Transmitted signals go to the first device and from the first to the second and so on.

daisy wheel Print mechanism that uses a plastic or metal hub with spokes like an old-fashioned wagon wheel minus the outer rim. At the end of each spoke is the carved image of a type character. This technology has been obsoleted by dot matrix and laser printers.

DASD (**D**irect **A**ccess **S**torage **D**evice) Pronounced "dazdee." Peripheral device that is directly addressable, such as a disk or drum.

DAT (1) (**D**igital **A**udio **T**ape) CD-quality, digital recording technology for magnetic tape. A 4mm, helical-scan DAT drive holds several gigabytes with extended-length tapes when adapted for data storage use. See *tape backup*.

(2) (**D**ynamic **A**ddress **T**ranslator) Hardware circuit that converts a virtual memory address into a real address.

data (1) Technically, raw facts and figures, such as orders and payments, which are processed into information, such as balance due and quantity on hand. However, in common usage, the terms data and information are used synonymously.

(2) Any form of information whether on paper or in electronic form. In electronic form, data refers to data fields, records, files and databases, word processing documents, raster and vector graphics images and digitally-encoded voice and video.

data administration Analysis, classification and maintenance of an organization's data and data relationships. It includes the development of data models and data dictionaries, which, combined with transaction volume, are the raw materials for database design.

data administrator Person who coordinates activities within the data administration department. Contrast with *database administrator*.

data bank Any electronic depository of data.

database (1) Set of interrelated files that is created and managed by a DBMS.

(2) Any electronically-stored collection of data.

database administrator Person responsible for the physical design and management of the database and for the evaluation, selection and implementation of the DBMS. In small organizations, the database administrator and data administrator are one in the same; however, when the two responsibilities are managed separately, the database administrator's function is more technical.

database management system See *DBMS*.

database manager (1) With personal computers, software that allows a user to manage multiple data files (same as *DBMS*). Contrast with *file manager*, which works with one file at a time.

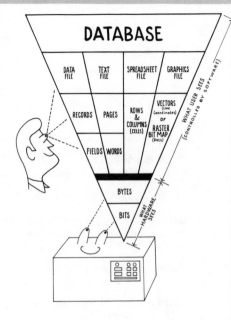

(2) Software that provides database management capability for traditional programming languages, such as COBOL, BASIC and C, but without the interactive capabilities.

(3) The part of the DBMS that stores and retrieves the data.

data bus Internal pathway across which data is transferred to and from the CPU. Personal computer expansion slots connect to the data bus.

data cartridge Removable magnetic tape module. See *QIC*.

data cassette Audio cassette made to higher tolerances for data storage.

datacenter Department that houses the computer systems and related equipment, including the data library. Data entry and systems programming may also come under its jurisdiction. A control section is usually provided that accepts work from and releases output to user departments.

data code (1) Digital coding system for data in a computer. The two major codes are ASCII and EBCDIC.

(2) Coding system used to abbreviate data, for example, codes for regions, classes, products and status.

data collection Acquiring source documents for data entry.

data communications Same as *communications*.

data compression Encoding data to take up less storage space. For example, short names in fixed length fields waste a lot of space. A simple method called *run length encoding* converts the spaces into a code that indicates how many blanks follow.

Text files can be compressed the most; for example, the text you're reading can be compressed from 50 to 70% depending on method used. Dense machine language files can be compressed about a third. Some graphics files leave little room for compaction, others compress well.

data control department Function responsible for collecting data for input into a computer's batch processing operations as well as the dissemination of the finished reports.

DATA/DAT (**DATA**/**D**igital **A**udio **T**ape) DAT format for data backup that can be divided into as many as 254 partitions allowing for updating in place. See *tape backup*.

data definition (1) In a source language program, the definitions of data structures (variables, arrays, fields, records, etc.).

(2) Description of the record layout in a file system or DBMS.

data dictionary Database about data and databases. It holds the name, type, range of values, source, and authorization for access for each data element in the organization's files and databases. It also indicates which application programs use that data so that when a change in a data structure is contemplated, a list of affected programs can be generated.

The data dictionary may be a stand-alone system or may be an integral part of, and used to control, the DBMS. Data integrity and accuracy is better insured in the latter case.

data dipper Software in a personal computer that queries a mainframe database.

data element Fundamental data structure in a data processing system. Any unit of data defined for processing is a data element; for example, ACCOUNT NUMBER, NAME, ADDRESS and CITY. A data element is defined by size (in characters) and type (alphanumeric, numeric only, true/false, date, etc.). A specific set of values or range of values may also be part of the definition.

Technically, a data element is a logical definition of data, whereas a field is the physical unit of storage in a record. For example, the data element ACCOUNT NUMBER, which exists only once, is stored in the ACCOUNT NUMBER field in the customer record, as well as the ACCOUNT NUMBER field in the order records.

Data element, data item, field and *variable* all describe the same unit of data and are used interchangeably.

data encryption See *encryption* and *DES*.

data entry Entering data into the computer, which includes keyboard entry, optical scanning and voice recognition.

data entry program Application program that accepts data from the keyboard or other input device and stores it in the computer.

data file Collection of data records. Contrast with *text file* and *graphics file*.

data flow (1) In computers, the path of data from source document to data entry to processing to final reports. Data changes format and sequence (within a file) as it moves from program to program.

(2) In communications, the path taken by a message from origination to destination and includes all nodes through which the data travels.

data flow diagram Description of data and the manual and machine processing performed on the data.

data glove Glove used to report the position of a user's hand and fingers to a computer. See *virtual reality*.

data independence DBMS technique that separates data from the processing and allows the database to be structurally changed without affecting existing programs.

data integrity Process of preventing accidental erasure or adulteration in a database.

data item Unit of data. See *field*.

data library Section of the datacenter that houses offline disks and tapes. Data library personnel are responsible for cataloging and maintaining the media.

DATA LIBRARY
DATA LIBRARY

data link protocol In communications, the transmission of a unit of data from one node to another. It is responsible for ensuring that the bits received are the same as the bits sent. See *communications protocol*.

data management Refers to several levels of managing data, from access methods to file managers and DBMSs to managing data as an organizational resource.

data management system See *DBMS*.

data model Description of the principles of organization of a database.

data modeling Identification of the design principles for a data model.

data module Sealed, removable storage module containing magnetic disks and their associated access arms and read/write heads.

data name Name assigned to an item of data, such as a field or variable.

data processing Capturing, storing, updating and retrieving data and information. It may refer to the entire computer industry or to data processing in contrast with other operations, such as word processing.

data processor (1) Person who works in data processing.

(2) Computer that is processing data, in contrast with a computer performing another task, such as controlling a network.

data projector Video machine that projects output from a computer onto a remote screen. It is bulkier than a flat LCD panel, but is faster for displaying high-speed animation.

data rate (1) Data transfer speed within the computer or between a peripheral and computer.

(2) Data transmission speed in a network.

data set (1) Data file or collection of interrelated data.

(2) AT&T name for modem.

data switch Switch box that routes one line to another; for example, to connect two computers to one printer. Manual switches have dials or buttons. Automatic switches test for signals and provide first-come, first-served switching.

data tablet Same as *digitizer tablet*.

data transparency Ability to easily access and work with data no matter where it is located or what application created it.

data type Category of data. Typical data types are numeric, alphanumeric (character), dates and logical (true/false). Programming languages allow for the creation of different data types.

date math Calculations on dates. For example, March 30 + 5 yields April 4.

datum Singular form of data; for example, one datum. It is rarely used, and data, its plural form, is commonly used for both singular and plural.

daughter board Small printed circuit board that is attached to or plugs into a removable printed circuit board.

dazdee See *DASD*.

DB See *database* and *decibel*.

DB-9, DB-15, DB-25, DB-37, DB-50 Category of plugs and sockets with 9, 15, 25, 37 and 50 pins respectively. DB refers to the physical structure of the connector, not the purpose of each line.

DB-9 and DB-25 connectors are commonly used for RS-232 interfaces. The DB-25 is also used on the computer end of the parallel printer cable for PCs (the printer end is a Centronics 36-pin connector).

A high-density DB-15 connector is used for the VGA port on a PC, which has 15 pins in the same shell as the DB-9 connector.

DB/DC (**D**ata**B**ase/**D**ata **C**ommunications) Refers to software that performs database and data communications functions.

DB-25 PLUG AND SOCKET

DB2 (**D**ata**B**ase 2) Relational DBMS from IBM that runs on large mainframes. It is a full-featured DBMS that has become IBM's major database product. It uses the SQL language interface.

DBA See *database administrator*.

dBASE Relational DBMS for PCs from Borland. It was the first comprehensive DBMS for personal computers and is still the most widely used. Originally marketed by Ashton-Tate, it provides an interactive database environment for the user and a programming language for developing complete applications. Its DBF file formats are de facto standards.

DBMS (**D**ata**B**ase **M**anagement **S**ystem) Software that controls the organization, storage, retrieval, security and integrity of data in a database. It accepts requests from the application and instructs the operating system to transfer the appropriate data.

DBMSs may be stand-alone systems that work with traditional programming languages, such as COBOL and C, or they may be complete development systems that include their own programming language and interactive capabilities for creating and managing databases, such as dBASE and Paradox.

DCE (1) (**D**ata **C**ommunications **E**quipment or **D**ata **C**ircuit-terminating **E**quipment) Typically a modem, it is a device that establishes a session on a network. Contrast with *DTE*.

(2) See *OSF*.

D/DAT See DATA/DATA.

DDE (**D**ynamic **D**ata **E**xchange) Message protocol in Windows that allows application programs to request and exchange data automatically. A program in one window can query a program in another window.

de facto standard Widely-used format or language not endorsed by a standards organization.

de jure standard Format or language endorsed by a standards organization.

deadlock See *deadly embrace*.

deadly embrace Stalemate that occurs when two elements in a process are each waiting for the other to respond. For example, in a network, if one user is working on file A and needs file B to continue, but another user is working on file B and needs file A to continue, each one waits for the other. Both are temporarily locked out. The software must be able to deal with this.

deallocate To release a computer resource that is currently assigned to a program or user, such as memory or a peripheral device.

deblock To separate records from a block.

debug To correct a problem in hardware or software. Debugging software is finding the errors in the program logic. Debugging hardware is finding the errors in circuit design.

debugger Software that helps a programmer debug a program by stopping at certain breakpoints and displaying various programming elements. The programmer can step through source code statements one at a time while the corresponding machine instructions are being executed.

DEC (**D**igital **E**quipment **C**orp.) Trade name for products (DECmate, DECnet, etc.). Many refer to the company as DEC. See *vendors*.

decay Reduction of strength of a signal or charge.

decentralized processing Computer systems in different locations. Although data may be transmitted between the computers periodically, it implies limited daily communications. Contrast with *distributed processing* and *centralized processing*.

decibel (dB) Unit that measures loudness or strength of a signal. A whisper is about 10 dB, a noisy factory 90 dB, loud thunder 110 dB. 120 dB is painful.

decimal Meaning 10. Universal numbering system that uses 10 digits. Computers use binary numbers because it is easier to design electronic systems that can maintain two states rather than 10.

decision box Diamond-shaped symbol that is used to document a decision point in a flowchart. The decision is written in the decision box, and the results of the decision branch off from the points in the box.

decision table List of decisions and their criteria. Designed as a matrix, it lists criteria (inputs) and the results (outputs) of all possible combinations of the criteria. It can be placed into a program to direct its processing. By changing the decision table, the program is changed accordingly.

INPUTS	OUTPUTS			
	APPROVE LOAN	DENY LOAN	SEE LOAN OFFICER	SEE LOAN OFFICER
SAME JOB OVER 5 YRS	YES	NO	NO	YES
OWNS CAR	YES	NO	YES	NO
OWNS HOME	YES	NO	YES	NO
IN DEBT	NO	YES	NO	NO

DECISION TABLE

decision tree Graphical representation of all alternatives in a decision making process.

deck (1) The part of a magnetic tape unit that holds and moves the tape reels.

(2) Set of punched cards.

(3) See DEC.

DECnet Digital's communications network, which supports Ethernet-style LANs and baseband and broadband WANs over private and public lines.

default Current setting or action taken by hardware or software if the user has not specified otherwise.

default directory Same as *current directory*.

default drive Disk drive used if no other drive is specified.

default font Typeface and type size used if none other is specified.

defragment To reorganize the disk by putting files back into a contiguous order.

degausser Device that removes unwanted magnetism from a monitor or the read/write head in a disk or tape drive.

delete To remove an item of data from a file or to remove a file from the disk. See *undelete*.

delimiter Character or combination of characters used to separate one item or set of data from another. For example, in comma delimited records, a comma is used to separate each field of data.

demodulate To filter out the data signal from the carrier. See *modulate*.

demon See *daemon*.

demultiplex To reconvert a transmission that contains several intermixed signals back into its original separate signals.

density See *bit density*.

DES (**D**ata **E**ncryption **S**tandard) NIST-standard encryption code for scrambling data.

descending sort Arranging data from high to low sequence (Z to A, 9 to 0).

descriptor (1) Word or phrase that identifies a document in an indexed information retrieval system.

(2) Category name used to identify data.

Designer Popular, full-featured Windows drawing program from Micrografx, Inc., Richardson, TX. It was the first PC program to provide almost all the design tools found in Macintosh drawing programs.

desk accessory In the Macintosh, a program that is always available no matter what application is running. With System 7, all applications can be turned into desk accessories.

desk checking Manually testing the logic of a program.

desktop (1) On-screen representation of a desktop. See *Macintosh* and *Windows*.

(2) Buzzword attached to applications traditionally performed on more expensive machines that are now on a personal computer (desktop publishing, desktop presentations, etc.).

desktop accessory Software that simulates an object normally found on an office desktop, such as a calculator, notepad and appointment calendar. It is typically RAM resident. See *TSR*.

desktop application See *desktop accessory*.

desktop computer Same as *personal computer* or *microcomputer*.

desktop media Integration of desktop presentations, desktop publishing and multimedia (coined by Apple).

desktop organizer See *desktop accessory*.

desktop presentations Creation of presentation materials on a personal computer, which includes charts, graphs and other graphics-oriented information.

desktop publishing Abbreviated "DTP." Using a personal computer to produce high-quality printed output or camera-ready output for commercial printing.

DESQview Popular multitasking, windows environment for DOS from Quarterdeck Office Systems, Santa Monica, CA. It runs multiple DOS text and graphics programs in resizable windows.

DESQview/X Version of DESQview that runs DOS, Windows and X Window applications locally or remotely on other DESQview/X PCs or X workstations. It allows DOS and Windows apps to run in an X Window network under UNIX or any other X-based environment.

developer's toolkit Set of software routines used in programming to link an application program to a particular operating environment (graphical user interface, operating system, DBMS, etc.).

development cycle See *system development cycle*.

device Electronic or electromechanical machine or component from a transistor to a disk drive. Device always refers to hardware.

device dependent Refers to programs that address specific hardware features and work with only one type of peripheral device. Contrast with *device independent*. See *machine dependent*.

device driver See *driver*.

device independent Refers to programs that work with a variety of peripheral devices. The hardware-specific instructions are in some other program (operating system, DBMS, etc.). Contrast with *device dependent*. See *machine independent*.

Dhrystones Benchmark program that tests a general mix of instructions. See *Whetstones*.

diagnostic board Expansion board with built-in diagnostic tests that reports results via its own readout. Boards for PCs have their own POST system and can test a malfunctioning computer that doesn't boot.

diagnostic tracks Spare tracks on a disk used by the drive or controller for testing purposes.

diagnostics (1) Software routines that test hardware components (memory, keyboard, disks, etc.). In personal computers, they are often stored in ROM and activated on startup.

(2) Error messages in a programmer's source code that refer to statements or syntax that the compiler or assembler cannot understand.

dial-up line Two-wire line as found in the dial-up network. Contrast with *leased line*.

dial-up network Switched telephone network regulated by government and administered by common carriers.

DIALOG See *online services*.

dialog box Small, on-screen window displayed in response to some request. It provides the options currently available to the user.

die Formal term for the square of silicon containing an integrated circuit. The popular term is chip.

DIF (1) (**D**ata **I**nterchange **F**ormat) Standard file format for spreadsheet and other data structured in row and column form. Originally developed for VisiCalc, DIF is now under Lotus' jurisdiction.

(2) (**D**ocument **I**nterchange **F**ormat) File standard developed by the U.S. Navy in 1982.

(3) (**D**ual **I**n-line **F**latpack) Type of surface mount DIP with pins extending horizontally outward.

digital (1) Traditionally, the use of numbers and comes from digit, or finger. Today, digital is synonymous with computer.

(2) (Digital Equipment Corp.) See *vendors*.

digital camera Video camera that records its images in digital form. Unlike traditional analog cameras that convert light intensities into infinitely variable signals, digital cameras convert light intensities into discrete numbers.

digital circuit Electronic circuit that accepts and processes binary data (on/off) according to the rules of Boolean logic.

Digital Equipment See *vendors*.

digital mapping Digitizing geographic information for a geographic information system (GIS).

Digital Research See *vendors*.

digital signal processing Category of techniques that analyze signals from a wide range of sources, such as voice, weather satellites and earthquake monitors. It converts the signals into digital data and analyzes it using various algorithms such as Fast Fourier Transform.

digital signature Coded message that can be verified by the receiver as being sent by an authentic sender.

digitize To convert an image or signal into digital code for the computer by scanning, tracing on a graphics tablet or by using an analog to digital conversion device.

digitizer tablet Graphics drawing tablet used for sketching new images or tracing old ones and for selecting from menus.

DIGITIZER TABLET

dimension One axis in an array. In programming, a dimension statement defines the array and sets up the number of elements within the dimensions.

dimensioning In CAD programs, the management and display of the measurements of an object. There are various standards that determine such things as tolerances, sizes of arrowheads and orientation on the paper.

DIN connector (**D**eutsches **I**nstitut für **N**ormung - German Standards Institute) Plug and socket used to connect a variety of devices; for example, the PC keyboard uses a five-pin DIN. DIN plugs look like an open metal can about a half inch in diameter with pins inside in a circular pattern.

dingbats Group of typesetting and desktop publishing symbols from International Typeface Corp. that include arrows, pointing hands, stars and circled numbers. They are formally called ITC Zapf Dingbats.

diode Electronic component that acts primarily as a one-way valve. They are used in changing AC to DC, in sensors and light emitters and in modulating devices for communications. They also serve as one-way valves in digital circuits.

DIP (**D**ual **I**n-line **P**ackage) Common rectangular chip housing with leads (pins) on both long sides. Tiny wires bond the chip to metal leads that wind their way down into spider-like feet that are inserted into a socket or are soldered onto the board.

DIP

DIP switch Tiny toggle switches built into a DIP, mounted on a circuit board. Remember! Open is "off." Closed is "on."

Dir (**DIR**ectory) CP/M, DOS and OS/2 command that lists the file names on the disk.

direct access Ability to go directly to a specific storage location without having to go through what's in front of it. Memories (RAMs, ROMs, PROMs, etc.) and disks are the major direct access devices.

DIP SWITCH

direct access method Technique for finding data on a disk by deriving its storage address from an identifying key in the record, such as account number. Using a formula, the account number is converted into a sector address, which is faster than comparing entries in an index. This method works best when keys are numerically close: 100, 101, 102.

directory Simulated file drawer on disk. Programs and data for each application are typically kept in a separate directory (spreadsheets, word processing, etc.). Directories create the illusion of compartments, but are actually indexes to the files which may be scattered all over the disk.

directory tree Graphic representation of a hierarchical directory.

dirty power Non-uniform AC power (voltage fluctuations, noise and spikes), which comes from the electric utility or from electronic equipment in the office.

disable To turn off a function. Disabled means turned off, not broken. Contrast with *enable*.

disc Alternate spelling for disk. Compact discs and videodiscs are spelled with the "c." Most computer disks are spelled with a "k."

discrete Component or device that is separate and distinct and treated as a singular unit.

discrete component Elementary electronic device constructed as a single unit. Before integrated circuits (chips), all transistors, resistors and diodes were discrete. They are widely used in high-power applications and are still used on circuit boards intermingled with the chips.

dish Saucer-shaped antenna that receives, or transmits and receives, signals from a satellite.

disk Direct access storage device. See *magnetic disk* and *optical disk*.

disk array Two or more disk drives combined in a single unit for increased capacity, speed and/or fault tolerant operation. See *RAID*.

disk based (1) Computer system that uses disks as its storage medium.

(2) Application that retrieves data from the disk as required. Contrast with *memory based*.

disk cache See *cache*.

disk cartridge Removable disk module that contains a single hard disk platter or a floppy disk.

DISK CARTRIDGES

disk controller Circuit that controls transmission to and from the disk drive. In a personal computer, it is an expansion board that plugs into an expansion slot in the bus. See *ESDI, IDE* and *SCSI*.

disk drive Peripheral storage device that holds, spins, reads and writes magnetic or optical disks. It may be a receptacle for disk cartridges, disk packs or floppy disks, or it may contain non-removable disk platters like most personal computer hard disks.

disk format Storage layout of a disk as determined by its physical medium and as initialized by a format program. For example, a 5.25" 360KB floppy vs a 3.5" 1.44MB floppy or a DOS disk vs a Mac disk. See *low-level format, high-level format* and *file format*.

disk management Maintenance and control of a hard disk. Refers to a variety of utilities that provide format, copy, diagnostic, directory management and defragmenting functions.

disk mirroring Recording of redundant data for fault tolerant operation. Data is written on two partitions of the same disk, on two separate disks within the same system or on two separate computer systems.

disk operating system See *DOS*.

disk pack Removable hard disk module used in minis and mainframes that contains two or more platters housed in a dust-free container. For mounting, the bottom of the container is removed. After insertion, the top is removed.

disk striping Spreading data over multiple disk drives. Data is interleaved by bytes or by sectors across the drives.

DISK PACKS

diskette Same as *floppy disk*.

diskless workstation Workstation without a disk. Programs and data are retrieved from the network server.

display adapter Same as *video display board*.

display list Collection of vectors that make up a vector graphics image.

display terminal See *video terminal*.

DisplayWrite IBM word processing program for PCs that stems from the typewriter-oriented DisplayWriter word processing system first introduced in 1980. See *XyWrite III Plus*.

distributed computing Same as *distributed processing*.

distributed database Database physically stored in two or more computer systems. Although geographically dispersed, a distributed database system manages and controls the entire database as a single collection of data. If redundant data is stored in separate databases, updates to one set will automatically update the additional sets in a timely manner.

distributed file system Software that keeps track of files stored across multiple networks. It converts file names into physical locations.

distributed processing System of computers connected together by a communications network. The term is loosely used to refer to any computers with communications between them. However, in true distributed processing, each computer system is chosen to handle its local workload, and the network has been designed to support the system as a whole. Contrast with *centralized processing* and *decentralized processing*.

dithering In computer graphics, the creation of additional colors and shades from an existing palette. In monochrome displays, shades of grays are created by varying the density and patterns of the dots. In color displays, colors and patterns are created by mixing and varying the dots of existing colors.

Dithering is used to create a wide variety of patterns for use as backgrounds, fills and shading, as well as for creating halftones for printing. It is also used in anti-aliasing.

DMA (**D**irect **M**emory **A**ccess) Specialized circuitry or a dedicated microprocessor that transfers data from memory to memory without using the CPU. Although DMA may periodically steal cycles from the CPU, data is transferred much faster than using the CPU for every byte of transfer.

docking station Base station for a laptop that includes a power supply and expansion slots as well as monitor and keyboard connectors.

docs Short for "documents" or "documentation."

document (1) Any paper form that has been filled in.

(2) Word processing text file.

(3) In the Macintosh, any text, data or graphics file that is created in the computer. In this book, document refers only to text files.

document handling Procedure for transporting and handling paper documents for data entry into scanning machines.

documentation Narrative and graphical description of a system.

domain (1) In database management, all possible values contained in a particular field for every record in the file.

(2) In communications, all the resources under control of a single computer system.

(3) In magnetic storage devices, a group of molecules that makes up one bit.

(4) In a hierarchy, a named group that has control over the groups under it, which may be domains themselves.

DOS (1) (**D**isk **O**perating **S**ystem) Pronounced "dahss." Generic term for operating system.

(2) (**D**isk **O**perating **S**ystem) Single-user operating system for the PC, PS/1 and PS/2 series from IBM. DOS is also called PC-DOS to distinguish it from MS-DOS, the version for non-IBM PCs. DOS and MS-DOS are developed by Microsoft, are almost identical, and both are referred to as DOS. IBM has participated in DOS development in varying degrees.
   In this book, DOS refers to both PC-DOS and MS-DOS.

DOS 5.0 Major DOS upgrade introduced in 1991 that includes an enhanced DOS shell with task swapping, a utility for restoring deleted files and formatted disks, a full-screen text editor and online help. It uses less memory by loading drivers and part of itself into high memory, and it supports 2GB hard disks and 2.88MB floppies.

DOS 6.0 Scheduled for 1993, successor to DOS 5.0, which includes realtime compression and improved memory management. New utilities are also provided.

DOS extender Software that is combined with a DOS application to allow it to run in extended memory (beyond 1MB). Some DOS extenders work with 286s and up, others require a 386 minimum.

DOS file (1) Any computer file created under DOS.

(2) ASCII text file.

DOS memory manager Software that manages extended memory and expanded memory (EMS) in a DOS PC. It allows TSRs and drivers to be moved out of the lower 640K and into the upper memory area (UMA). In 386s and up, it turns extended memory into EMS memory and may be able to automatically allocate both kinds of memory on demand.

DOS prompt Message DOS displays when ready to accept user input. The default prompt (C:>, D:>...) displays the current drive but not the current directory. PCs are usually configured with a **prompt pg** line in the AUTOEXEC.BAT file, which adds the directory name; for example: C:\BUDGETS>.

DOS shell Shells provide the user interface in DOS, or the way you interact with the system. COMMAND.COM is the program that provides the command-driven user interface. COMMAND.COM can be substituted with the shells that come with DOS 4.0 and 5.0 as well as third-party shells from many vendors.

dot matrix Pattern of dots that form character and

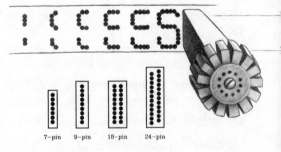

7-pin   9-pin   18-pin   24-pin

DOT MATRIX PRINTER PIN CONFIGURATIONS

graphic images on video screens and printers. Display screens use a matrix (rows and columns) of dots just like TVs. Serial printers use one or two columns of dot hammers that are moved across the paper. Laser printers "paint" dots of light a line at a time onto a light-sensitive photographic drum. The more dots per square inch, the higher the resolution of the characters and graphics.

dot pitch Distance between a red (or green or blue) dot and the closest red (or green or blue) dot on a color monitor (typically from .28 to .51mm; large presentation monitors may go up to 1.0mm). The smaller the dot pitch, the crisper the image. A dot pitch of .31 or less provides a sharp image, especially on text.

double click To press the mouse button twice in rapid succession.

double density disk Floppy disk with twice the capacity of the prior format. It originally meant high density; now it means low density. The 5.25" 360KB and 3.5" 720KB floppies are examples.

download To transmit a file from one computer to another. When conducting the session, download means receive, upload means transmit. It implies sending a block of data rather than interacting in a conversational mode.

downloadable font Same as *soft font*.

downsizing Converting mainframe and mini-based systems to personal computer LANs.

downtime Time during which a computer is not functioning due to hardware or system software failure. That's when you truly understand how important it is to have reliable hardware.

downward compatible Also called backward compatible. Refers to hardware or software that is compatible with earlier versions. Contrast with *upward compatible*.

DP See *data processing* and *dot pitch*.

dpi (**D**ots **P**er **I**nch) Measurement of printer resolution. A 300 dpi printer means 90,000 dots are printable in one square inch (300x300).

DR DOS (**D**igital **R**esearch DOS) DOS-compatible operating system from Novell noted for its many features. Version 5.0 includes built-in help, passwords, disk cache, serial port file transfer, the ability to store itself and drivers in high memory and an optional graphical interface. Version 6.0 includes file compression that doubles hard disk space.

draft mode Highest-speed, lowest-quality printing mode.

drag To move an object on screen in which its complete movement is visible from starting location to destination. The movement may be activated with a stylus, mouse or keyboard keys.

drag & drop Ability to execute a function graphically without typing in a command. For example, in the Macintosh, selecting a floppy disk icon and dragging it onto the trashcan icon causes the floppy to be ejected.

DRAM, D-RAM See *dynamic RAM*.

drawing program Graphics software that allows the user to design and illustrate products and objects. It maintains an image in vector graphics format, which allows all elements of the graphic object to be isolated and manipulated individually.

Drawing programs and CAD programs are similar; however, drawing programs usually provide a large number of special effects for fancy illustrations, while CAD programs provide precise dimensioning and positioning of each graphic element in order that the objects can be transferred to other systems for engineering analysis and manufacturing. Contrast with *paint program*.

drill down To move from summary information to the detailed data that created it.

drive (1) Electromechanical device that spins disks and tapes at a specified speed. Also refers to the entire peripheral unit such as *disk drive* or *tape drive*.

(2) To provide power and signals to a device. For example, "this control unit can drive up to 15 terminals."

drive bay Slot for a disk drive in a computer cabinet.

drive door Panel, gate or lever used to lock a disk in a disk drive. In a 5.25" floppy drive, the drive door is the lever that is turned down over the slot after inserting the disk.

driver (1) Also called a *device driver*, a program routine that links a peripheral device or internal function to the operating system. It contains the precise machine language necessary to activate all device functions and includes detailed knowledge of its characteristics, such as sectors per track or the number of pixels of screen resolution.

(2) Device that provides signals or electrical current to activate a transmission line or display screen.

DS/DD (**D**ouble **S**ided/**D**ouble **D**ensity) Refers to floppy disks, such as the 5.25" 360KB PC format and 3.5" 720KB PC and 800KB Mac formats.

DS/HD (**D**ouble **S**ided/**H**igh **D**ensity) Refers to floppy disks, such as the 5.25" 1.2MB PC format and 3.5" 1.44MB PC and Mac formats.

DSS (**D**ecision **S**upport **S**ystem) Information and planning system that provides the ability to interrogate computers on an ad hoc basis, analyze information and predict the impact of decisions before they are made. See *EIS*.

DTE (**D**ata **T**erminating **E**quipment) Typically a terminal or computer, it is a communications device that is the source or destination of signals on a network. Contrast with *DCE*.

DTP See *desktop publishing*.

dual boot Computer that can be started with either one of two different operating systems.

dual in-line package See *DIP*.

dumb terminal Display terminal without processing capability. It is entirely dependent on the main computer for processing. Contrast with *smart terminal* and *intelligent terminal*.

dump To print the contents of memory, disk or tape without any report formatting. See *memory dump*.

duplex channel See *full-duplex*.

duplexed system Two systems that are functionally identical. They both may perform the same functions, or one may be standby, ready to take over if the other fails.

duplicate keys Identical key data in a file. Primary keys, such as account number cannot be duplicated, since no two customers or employees should be assigned the same number. Secondary keys, such as date, product and city, may be duplicated in the file or database.

DVI (**D**igital **V**ideo **I**nteractive) Intel compression technique for data, audio and full-motion video. On a CD ROM, it provides up to 72 minutes of full-screen video, 2 hours of half-screen video, 40,000 medium-resolution or 7,000 high-resolution images. It compresses full-motion video at ratios greater than 100 to 1 and still images at 10 to 1.

Split screen capabilities allow still and moving images side by side. For example, a training course could show an operation taking place along with pictures of the components being used.

Dvorak keyboard
Keyboard layout designed in the 1930s by August Dvorak, University of Washington, and his brother-in-law, William Dealey. 70% of words are typed on the home row compared to 32% with qwerty, and, more words are typed using both hands. In eight hours, fingers of a qwerty typist travel 16 miles, but only one for the Dvorak typist.

DVORAK KEYBOARD LAYOUT

DX See 386 and 486.

DX2 See 486.

dyadic Two. Refers to two components being used.

dynamic Refers to operations performed while the program is running. The expression, "buffers are dynamically created," means that space was created when actually needed, not reserved beforehand.

dynamic RAM Most common type of computer memory, also called D-RAM ("dee-RAM") and DRAM. It usually uses one transistor and a capacitor to represent a bit. The capacitors must be energized hundreds of times per second in order to maintain the charges. Unlike firmware chips (ROMs, PROMs, etc.) both major varieties of RAM (dynamic and static) lose their content when the power is turned off. Contrast with *static* RAM.

In memory ads, dynamic RAM is often erroneously mentioned as a package type; for example, "DRAMs, SIMMs and SIPs on sale." It should be "DIPs, SIMMs and SIPs," as all three packages typically hold dynamic RAM chips.

dynamic range Range of signals from the weakest to the strongest.

earth station Transmitting/receiving station for satellite communications. It uses a dish-shaped antenna for microwave transmission.

EBCDIC (Extended Binary Coded Decimal Interchange Code) Pronounced "eb-suh-dick." Data code used in IBM mainframes and most midrange computers. It is an 8-bit code (256 combinations) that stores one alphanumeric character or two decimal digits within a byte. EBCDIC and ASCII are the primary methods for coding data.

EDI (Electronic Data Interchange) Electronic communication of transactions between organizations, such as orders, confirmations and invoices.

edit To make a change to existing data. See *update*.

edit checking Same as *validity checking*.

editor See *text editor*.

EDP (Electronic Data Processing) First name used for the computer field.

EEPROM (Electrically Erasable Programmable Read Only Memory) Memory chip that holds its content without power. It can be erased, either within the computer or externally and usually requires more voltage for erasure than the common +5 volts used in logic circuits.

EGA (Enhanced Graphics Adapter) IBM video display standard that provides medium-resolution text and graphics. It has been superseded by VGA.

EIS (Executive Information System) Information system that consolidates and summarizes ongoing transactions within the organization. It should provide management with all the information it requires at all times from internal as well as external sources. See *DSS*.

EISA (Extended ISA) Pronounced "e-suh." PC bus standard that extends the AT bus (ISA bus) to 32 bits and provides bus mastering. It was announced in 1988 as a 32-bit alternative to the Micro Channel that would preserve investment in existing boards. PC and AT cards (ISA cards) can plug into an EISA slot.

electroluminescent Flat panel display that provides a sharp, clear image and wide viewing angle. It uses a phospher that typically glows amber or green.

electronic Use of electricity in intelligence-bearing devices, such as radios, TVs, instruments, computers and telecommunications. Electricity used as raw power for heat, light and motors is considered electrical, not electronic.

electronic mail Transmission of memos and messages over a network. E-mail systems are implemented in mainframe, mini and personal computer LANs.

electrophotographic Printing technique used in copy machines and laser printers. A negative image made of dots of light is painted onto a photosensitive drum or belt that has been electrically charged. Wherever light is applied, the drum becomes uncharged. A toner (dry ink) is applied and adheres to the charged areas of the drum. The drum transfers the toner to the paper, and pressure and heat fuse the toner and paper permanently.

e-mail See *electronic mail.*

embedded system Specialized computer used to control a device such as an automobile, appliance or space vehicle.

EMI (**E**lectro**M**agnetic **I**nterference) Electromagnetic waves that eminate from an electrical device. It often refers to both low-frequency waves from electromechanical devices and high-frequency waves (RFI) from chips and other electronic devices. Allowable limits are governed by the FCC.

EMM (**E**xpanded **M**emory **M**anager) Software that manages expanded memory (EMS). In XTs and ATs, expanded memory boards must be used. In 386s and up, the EMM converts extended memory into EMS.

EMS (**E**xpanded **M**emory **S**pecification) Technique for increasing memory in DOS PCs up to 32MB. It stretches conventional memory (the memory DOS can work with) by switching segments of EMS memory into the conventional memory area as needed.

In XTs and ATs, EMS is installed by plugging in an EMS memory board and adding an EMS driver. In 386s and up, EMS is created by expanded memory manager (EMM) software that turns extended memory into EMS.

In order to use EMS, the application is either written to use it directly (Lotus 1-2-3 Ver. 2.x, AutoCAD, etc.) or the application is run in an environment that uses it, such as DESQview.

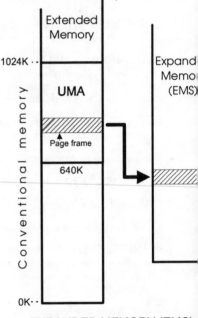

EXPANDED MEMORY (EMS)

DOS can only reach the first megabyte of me (conventional memory). When EMS is used, a chunk of the UMA (upper memory area) is reserve the EMS page frame, which serves as a window int EMS memory bank. Circuits on the EMS board r the requested 64K EMS area into the page frame which DOS can address.

Expanded Memory vs Extended Memory

Expanded memory (EMS) and extended memory are not the same. EMS can be installed in XT-class machines and up, whereas extended memory requires at least a 286. EMS broke the 1MB memory barrier in the early days, however, now that 286s are the low-end CPU, extended memory is finally being utilized due to the widespread use of Windows 3.x and DOS-extended applications.

emulator Device that is built to work like another. A computer can be designed to emulate another model and execute software that was written to run in the other machine. A terminal can be designed to emulate various communications protocols and connect to different networks. The emulator can be hardware, software or both.

enable To turn on. Contrast with *disable*.

encryption Encoding data for security purposes by converting it into a proprietary code. See *DES*.

end user Same as *user*.

endless loop Series of instructions that are constantly repeated. It can be caused by an error in the program or it can be intentional; for example, a screen demo on continuous replay.

engine (1) Specialized processor, such as a graphics processor. Like any engine, the faster it runs, the quicker the job gets done.

(2) Software that performs a primary and highly repetitive function such as a database engine, graphics engine or dictionary engine.

enter key See *return key*.

enterprise network Geographically-dispersed network under the jurisdiction of one organization that typically contains systems from several vendors.

entity In a database, anything about which information can be stored; for example, a person, concept, physical object or event. Typically refers to a record structure.

entity relationship model In a database, a data model that describes attributes of entities and the relationships among them.

environment Computer configuration that includes the CPU model and system software (operating system, data communications and database systems). It sets the standards for the applications that run in it. It may also include the programming language used. The term often refers only to the operating system; for example, "This program is running in a UNIX environment."

EPROM (**E**rasable **P**rogrammable **ROM**) Reusable PROM chip that holds its content until erased under ultraviolet light. See *PROM programmer*.

Epson emulation Compatible with Epson dot matrix printers. The command set in the Epson MX, RX and FX printers has become an industry standard.

EPSS (**E**lectronic **P**erformance **S**upport **S**ystem) Computer system that provides quick assistance and information without requiring prior training to use it. It may incorporate all forms of multimedia delivery as well as AI techniques such as expert systems and natural language recognition.

ergonomics Science of people-machine relationships. An ergonomically-designed product implies that the device blends smoothly with a person's body or actions.

error checking (1) Testing for accurate transmission of data over a communications network or internally within the computer system. See *parity checking* and *CRC*.

(2) Same as *validity checking*.

error control Same as *error checking*.

error detection & correction See *error checking* and *validity checking*.

error-free channel Interface (wire, cable, etc.) between devices that is not subject to external interference; specifically not the dial-up telephone system.

error handling Routines in a program that respond to errors. The measurement of quality in error handling is based on how the system informs the user of such conditions and what alternatives it provides for dealing with them.

error rate Measurement of the quality of a communications channel. It is the ratio of the number of erroneous units of data found in the total number of units sent.

ES/9000 See IBM *mainframes*.

esc See *escape key* and *escape character*.

escape character Control character often used in conjunction with other codes. For example, an escape, followed by **&l1o**, sets the HP LaserJet to landscape mode. In ASCII, escape is decimal 27, hex 1B.

escape key Commonly used key to exit or cancel the current mode or operation.

escape sequence Machine command that starts with an escape character. Printers are often commanded by escape sequences. See *escape character*.

ESDI (**E**nhanced **S**mall **D**evice **I**nterface) Hard disk interface that transfers data in the one to three MByte/sec range. ESDI has always been known as the high-quality, high-speed interface for small computers. IDE drives now incorporate similar technology and are beginning to rival ESDI performance.

Ethernet Local area network (IEEE 802.3) that transmits at 10Mbits/sec and can connect up to 1,024 nodes in total. Standard Ethernet or "thick Ethernet" (10Base5) uses a bus topology with a maximum segment length of 1,640 ft. and 100 devices. Thin Ethernet or "ThinNet" or "CheaperNet" (10Base2) uses a bus topology with a segment length of 607 feet and 30 devices. Twisted pair Ethernet (10BaseT) uses telephone wire and connects two devices per segment up to 328 feet. Fiber Optic Ethernet (10BaseF) extends the distance to 1.3 miles and is impervious to external radiation. The latter two methods use a star topology, considered easier to debug as networks expand.

event driven Application that responds to input from the user or other application at unregulated times. It's driven by choices that the user makes (select menu, press button, etc.).

Excel Full-featured spreadsheet for PCs and the Macintosh from Microsoft. It can link many spreadsheets for consolidation and provides a wide variety of business graphics and charts for creating presentation materials.

exception report Listing of abnormal items or items that fall outside of a specified range.

EXE file (**EXE**cutable file) Runnable program in DOS, OS/2 and VMS. In DOS, if a program fits within 64K, it may be a COM file.

executable Program in machine language that is ready to run in a particular computer environment.

execute To follow instructions in a program. Same as *run*.

execution time Time in which a single instruction is executed.

executive Same as *operating system*.

exit (1) To get out of the current mode or quit the program.

(2) In programming, to get out of the loop, routine or function that the computer is currently in.

expanded memory See *EMS and EMM*.

expanded memory emulator Memory manager for 386s and up that converts extended memory into EMS memory. See *EMM*.

expansion board (1) Printed circuit board that plugs into an expansion slot.

(2) See *bus extender*.

expansion bus The computer's bus comprised of a series of receptacles or slots into which expansion boards (video display, disk controller, etc.) are plugged.

expansion slot Receptacle inside a computer or other electronic system that accepts printed circuit boards. The number of slots determines future expansion. In personal computers, expansion slots are connected to the bus.

expert system AI application that uses a knowledge base of human expertise for problem solving. Its success is based on the quality of the data and rules obtained from the human expert. In practice, expert systems perform both below and above that of a human.

export To convert a data file created by the current application program into a format required by another application program.

expression In programming, a statement that describes data and processing. For example, `value=2*cost` and `product="hat" and color="gray"`.

extended ASCII Second half of the ASCII character set (128 through 255). The symbols are defined by ANSI, by IBM for the PC and by other vendors for proprietary uses. It is non-standard ASCII.

extended memory Memory above one megabyte in 286s and up. See "Expanded Memory vs Extended Memory" in *EMS*.

extensible Capable of being expanded.

extension DOS and OS/2 file category added to the end of the file name with a dot. An extension can have up to three letters or digits; for example, executable files use .EXE, .COM and .BAT extensions.

 All programs and most data files use extensions. However, some word processing files do not, in which case you could create your own filing system; for example, CHAP1.NOV and CHAP2.NOV could be chapters in a novel.

facilities management Management of a user's computer installation by an outside organization. All operations including systems, programming and the datacenter can be performed by the facilities management organization on the user's premises.

Fast Fourier Transform Class of algorithms used in digital signal processing that break down complex signals into elementary components.

fatal error Condition that halts processing due to read errors, program bugs or anomalies.

fault tolerant Continous operation in case of failure. A fault tolerant system can be created using two or more computers that duplicate all processing, or having one system stand by if the other fails. It can also be built with redundant processors, control units and peripherals architecturally integrated from the ground up (Tandem, Stratus, etc.).

fax board Fax transmission on an expansion board. It uses software that generates fax signals directly from disk files or the screen and transmits a sharper image than a fax machine, which gets its image by scanning. Incoming faxes are printed on the computer's printer.

fax/modem Combination fax board and data modem available as an external unit or expansion board. It includes a fax switch that routes the call to the fax or the data modem.

FCC Class FCC certification of radiation limits on digital devices. Class A certification is for business use. Class B for residential use is more stringent in order to avoid interference with TV and other home reception. See Part 15, Subpart B, of the Federal Register (CFR 47, Parts 0-19).

FDDI (**F**iber **D**istributed **D**ata **I**nterface)   ANSI-standard, high-speed LAN that uses optical fiber cabling and transmits at 100 Mbits/sec up to 62 miles. FDDI specifications deal with OSI layers 1 and 2.

FDM (**F**requency **D**ivision **M**ultiplexing)   Method used to transmit multiple signals over a single channel. Each signal (data, voice, etc.) modulates a carrier with a different frequency and all signals travel simultaneously over the channel. Contrast with *TDM*. See *baseband*.

FDX See *full-duplex*.

feasibility study Analysis of a problem to determine if it can be solved effectively. The operational (will it work?), economical (costs and benefits) and technical (can it be built?) aspects are part of the study. Results of the study determine whether the solution should be implemented.

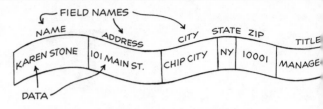

field Physical unit of data that is one or more bytes in size. A collection of fields make up a record. A field also defines a unit of data on a source document, screen or report. Examples of fields are NAME, ADDRESS, QUANTITY and AMOUNT DUE.

FIELDS IN A RECORD

The field is the common denominator between the user and the computer. When you interactively query and update your database, you reference your data by field name.

A field is the physical unit of storage, whereas a data item refers to the data itself. For example, the data items Chicago, Dallas and Phoenix are stored in the CITY field. The terms *field, data element, data item* and *variable* refer to the same unit of data and are often used interchangeably.

field engineer Person who is responsible for hardware installation, maintentance and repair. Formal training is in electronics, although many people have learned on the job.

field name Assigned name for a field (NAME, ADDRESS, CITY, STATE, etc.) that is the same in every record.

field separator Comma, tab or other character used to mark the separation of fields in a record. See *comma delimited*.

field service See *field engineer*.

field squeeze In a mail merge, a function that eliminates extra blanks between words when fixed-length fields are inserted into the document text. See *line squeeze*.

fifth-generation computer Computer designed for AI applications. Appearing in the late 1990s, these systems will represent the next technology leap.

file (1) In data management, a collection of related records.

(2) In word processing, a single text document.

(3) In computer graphics, a set of image descriptors for one picture, either in TV-like format (raster graphics) or in line, or object, format (vector graphics).

(4) In programming, the source program and machine language program are stored as individual *files*.

(5) In computer operations, any collection of data that is treated as a single unit on a peripheral device, such as any of the examples in items 1 through 4 above.

file and record locking First-come, first-served technique for managing data in a multiuser environment. The first user to access the file or record prevents, or locks out, other users from accessing it. After the file or record is updated, it is unlocked and available.

file attribute File access classification that allows a file to be retrieved or erased. Typical attributes are read/write, read only, archive and hidden.

file format Structure of a file. There are hundreds of proprietary formats for database, word processing and graphics files. See *record layout*.

file layout Same as *record layout*.

file maintenance (1) Periodic updating of master files. For example, adding/deleting employees and customers, making address changes and changing product prices. It does not refer to daily transaction processing and batch processing (order processing, billing, etc.).

(2) Periodic reorganization of the disk drives. Data that is continuously updated becomes physically fragmented over the disk space and requires regrouping. An optimizing program is run (daily, weekly, etc.) that rewrites all files contiguously.

file manager (1) Software that manages data files. Often erroneously called database managers, file managers provide the ability to create, enter, change, query and produce reports on one file at a time. They have no relational capabilty and usually don't include a programming language.

(2) Software used to manage files on a disk. It provides functions to delete, copy, move, rename and view files as well as create and manage directories.

file name Name assigned by the user or programmer that is used to identify a file.

file protect ring Plastic ring inserted into a reel of magnetic tape for file protection.

file protection Preventing accidental erasing of data. Physical file protection is provided on the storage medium by turning a switch, moving a lever, covering a notch or inserting a ring into a tape reel. Logical file protection is provided by the operating system, which can designate a single file as read only. This method allows both regular (read/write) and read only files to be stored on the same disk volume. Files can also be designated as hidden, which makes them invisible to most software programs.

file recovery program Software that recovers disk files that have been accidentally deleted or damaged.

file server High-speed computer in a LAN that stores the programs and data files shared by users on the network. Also called a network server, it acts like a remote disk drive.

file size Length of a file in bytes.

file spec (file **SPEC**ification) Reference to the location of a file on a disk, which includes disk drive, directory name and file name. For example, in DOS and OS/2, `c:\wordstar\books\chapter` is a file spec for the file CHAPTER in the BOOKS subdirectory in the WORDSTAR directory on drive C.

file viewer Software that displays the contents of a file as it would be normally displayed by the application that created it. It is usually capable of displaying a variety of common formats.

fill (1) In a paint program, to change the color of a bordered area.

(2) In a spreadsheet, to enter common or repetitive values into a group of cells.

fill pattern (1) Color, shade or pattern used to fill an area of an image.

(2) Signals transmitted by a LAN station when not receiving or transmitting data in order to maintain synchronization.

film recorder Device that takes a 35mm slide picture from a graphics file, which has been created in a CAD, paint or business graphics package. It generates very high resolution, typically 2,000 to 4,000 lines.

filter (1) Process that changes data, such as a sort routine that changes the sequence of items or a conversion routine (import or export filter) that changes one data, text or graphics format into another.

(2) Pattern or mask through which only selected data is passed. For example, in dBASE, `set filter to file overdue`, compares all data to the matching conditions stored in OVERDUE.

financial planning system Software that helps the user evaluate alternatives. It is a step above spreadsheets by providing additional analysis tools; however, some of these capabilities are being added to spreadsheets. For example, sensitivity analysis assigns a range of values to a data element, which causes that data to be highlighted if it ever exceeds that range.

　　　Goal seeking provides automatic calculation. For example, by entering `gross margin = 50%` as well as the minimums and maximums of the various inputs, the program will calculate an optimum mix of inputs to achieve the goal (output).

fingerprint reader Scanner used to identify a person's fingerprint for security purposes.

firmware Category of memory chips that hold their content without electrical power and include ROM, PROM, EPROM and EEPROM technologies. Firmware becomes "hard software" when holding program code.

first-generation computer Computer that used vacuum tubes as switching elements; for example, the UNIVAC I.

fixed disk Non-removable hard disk such as is found in most personal computers. Programs and data are copied to and from the fixed disk.

fixed-frequency monitor Monitor that accepts one type of video signal, such as VGA. Contrast with *multiscan monitor*.

fixed head disk Direct access storage device, such as a disk or drum, that has a read/write head for each track. Since there is no access arm movement, access times are significantly improved.

fixed length field Constant field size; for example, a 25-byte name field takes up 25 bytes in each record. Contrast with *variable length field*.

fixed length record Data record that contains fixed length fields.

fixed point Method for storing and calculating numbers in which the decimal point is always in the same location. Contrast with *floating point*.

Fkey (Function **key**) Macintosh command sequence using command, shift and option key combinations. For example, Fkey 1 (command-shift 1) ejects the internal floppy.

flag (1) In communications, a code in the transmitted message which indicates that the following characters are a control code and not data.

(2) In programming, a "yes/no" indicator built into certain hardware or created and controlled by the programmer.

flame Slang for communicating emotionally and/or excessively via electronic mail.

flash memory Memory chip that holds its content without power, but must be erased in bulk. As future designs provide for less-than-whole-chip erasure, and ultimately, byte by byte erasure, flash memory may provide an alternative to current-day RAM.

flat file Stand-alone data file that does not have any pre-defined linkages or pointers to locations of data in other files.

flat panel display Thin display screen that uses any of a number of technologies, such as LCD, electroluminscent or gas plasma.

flatbed plotter Graphics plotter that draws on sheets of paper that have been placed in a bed. The size of the bed determines the maximum size sheet that can be drawn.

flexible disk Same as *floppy disk*.

flip-flop Electronic circuit that alternates between two states.

floating point Method for storing and calculating numbers in which the decimal points don't line up as in fixed point numbers. The significant digits are stored as a unit called the mantissa, and the location of the radix point (decimal point in base 10) is stored in a separate unit called the exponent. Floating point methods are used for calculating a large range of numbers quickly.
Floating point operations can be implemented in hardware (math coprocessor), or they can be done in software.

MANTISSA	EXPONENT		ACTUAL VALUE
6508	0	=	6508
6508	1	=	65080
6508	-1	=	650.8

FLOATING POINT

floating point processor Arithmetic unit designed to perform floating point operations.

floppy disk Reusable magnetic storage medium. Also called a diskette. It is the primary method for distributing personal computer software. It's also used to transfer data between users, although local area networks eliminate much of this "sneakernet."
The two major formats are the 5.25" square envelope and the 3.5" rigid cartridge. It uses a flexible disk with a magnetic recording surface like tape. The disk drive grabs the floppy's center and spins it inside its housing, and the read/write head makes contact with the surface through an opening in the floppy's envelope, case or cartridge.

Although floppy disks look the same, what's recorded on them determines their capacity and compatibility. Each new floppy must be "formatted," which records the sectors on the disk that will hold the data. PC, Mac, Apple II, Amiga and Atari formats are different, although most can read and write PC (DOS) diskettes. See *format program* and *Floptical*.

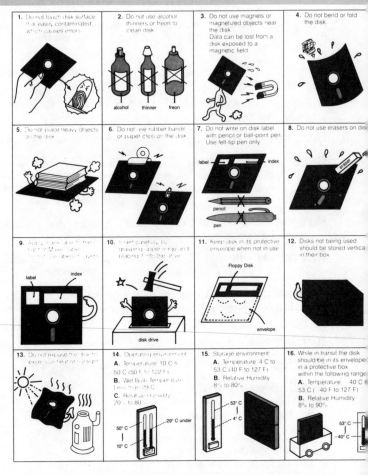

FLOPS
(**FL**oating point **O**perations **P**er **S**econd) Unit of measurement of floating point calculations. For example, 100 megaflops is 100 million floating point operations per second.

FLOPPY DISK HANDLING AND STORAGE
(Courtesy Maxell Corporation)

Floptical disk Floppy disk from Insite Peripherals, Inc., San Jose, CA, that records data magnetically, but uses grooves in the disk to optically align the head over the tracks. The first 3.5" Floptical drive uses 21MB diskettes and can also read and write 720K and 1.44MB disks.

flow chart Graphical representation of the sequence of operations in an information system or program.

flow control (1) In communications, the management of data transmission. It ensures that the receiving station can process the data before the next block is sent.

(2) In programming, the if-then and loop statements that make up the program's logic.

flush To empty the contents of a memory buffer onto disk.

Computer Words You Gotta Know

FM (**F**requency **M**odulation) Transmission technique that blends the data signal into a carrier by varying (modulating) the frequency of the carrier. See *modulate*.

Fn key (**F**u**N**ction key) Keyboard key that works like a shift key to activate the second function on a dual-purpose key, typically found on laptops to reduce keyboard size. It is different than the function keys F1, F2, etc.

folder In the Macintosh, a simulated file folder that holds documents (text, data or graphics), applications and other folders. A folder is like a DOS directory. A folder within a folder is like a DOS subdirectory.

font Set of type characters of a particular typeface design and size. Each typeface (Times Roman, Helvetica, etc.) generally includes normal weight and bold, italic and bold italic variations of the typeface, which constitute four fonts. See *bitmapped font* and *scalable font*.

font cartridge Set of bitmapped or outline fonts for one or more typefaces contained in a plug-in module for the printer. The fonts are stored in a ROM chip within the cartridge. Contrast with *soft font* and *internal font*.

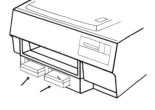

font compiler Same as *font generator*.

font editor Software that allows fonts to be designed and modified.

FONT CARTRIDGE

font family Set of fonts of the same typeface in assorted sizes, including bold, italic and bold italic variations.

font generator Software that converts an outline font into a bitmap (dot pattern required for a particular font size). Font generation implies creating fonts in advance of printing and storing them on disk. Font scaling implies creating fonts on the fly. See *font scaler*.

font metric Typographic information (width, height, kerning) for each character in a font.

font scaler Software that converts scalable fonts into bitmaps on the fly as required for display or printing. Examples are TrueType, Adobe Type Manager and Bitstream's Facelift. See *font generator* and *scalable font*.

font style Typeface variation (normal, bold, italic, bold italic).

footprint Amount of geographic space covered by an object. A satellite's footprint is the geographic area covered by its transmission to earth (downlink).

foreground/background Priority assigned to programs running in a multitasking environment. Foreground programs have highest priority, and background programs have lowest. Online users are given the foreground, and batch processing activities (sorts, updates, etc.) are given the background. See *background processing*.

format Structure, or layout, of an item. Screen formats are fields on the screen. Report formats are columns, headers and footers on a page.

Record formats are the fields within a record. File formats are the structure of data files, word processing documents and graphics files (display lists and bitmaps) and all associated codes.

format program Software that initializes a disk. There are two formatting levels. The low-level initializes the disk surface by creating the physical tracks and storing sector identification in them. Low-level format programs are geared to the drive technology used (IDE, SCSI, etc.).

The high-level format lays out the indexes used by the operating system (DOS, Mac, etc.) to keep track of data stored in the sectors.

Floppy disk format programs perform both levels on a diskette.

FORTRAN See *programming languages*.

fourth-generation computer Computer made up almost entirely of chips with limited amounts of discrete components. We are currently in the fourth generation.

fourth-generation language Computer language that is more advanced than traditional programming languages. For example, in dBASE, the command LIST displays all the records in a data file. Query programs and report writers are also examples.

FoxBASE+, FoxPro Fox programs are dBASE-compatible DBMSs for the Macintosh and PC from Microsoft. Originally developed by Fox Software, Fox database software is known for its speed and compatibility.

fps (1) (**F**rames **P**er **S**econd) See *frame*.

(2) (FPS) (**F**loating **P**oint **S**ystems, Inc., Beaverton, OR) Supercomputer manufacturer.

FPU (**F**loating **P**oint **U**nit) Computer circuit that handles floating point operations.

fractals Technique for describing and greatly compressing images, especially natural objects, such as trees, clouds and rivers. Fractals, or fractional mathematics, comes from the science of "chaos." It turns an image into a set of data and an algorithm for expanding it back to the original.

fractional T1 Service that provides less than full T1 capacity. One or more 64Kbps subchannels are provided.

fragmentation Non-contiguous storage of data on disk. As files are updated, new data is stored in available free space, which may not be contiguous. Fragmented files cause extra head movement, slowing disk accesses. A disk maintenance, or optimizer, program is used to rewrite and reorder all the files.

frame (1) In computer graphics, one screenful of data or its equivalent storage space.

(2) In communications, a group of bits that make up an elementary block of data for transmission by certain protocols.

(3) In AI, a data structure that holds a general description of an object, which is derived from basic concepts and experience.

frame buffer Separate memory component that holds a graphic image. It can have one plane of memory for each bit in the pixel; for example, if eight bits are used per pixel, there are eight separate memory planes.

frame grabber Device that converts video images into the computer. The frame grabber accepts standard TV signals and digitizes the current video frame into a computer graphics image.

frame relay High-speed packet switching protocol that provides faster transmission than X.25. It is suited for data and image transfer rather than voice.

FrameMaker Desktop publishing program from Frame Technology Corp., San Jose, CA, that runs on UNIX platforms, Macintosh and Windows. It is noted for its integrated text and graphics capabilities.

frequency division multiplexing See FDM.

frequency modulation See FM.

front end processor Computer that handles communications processing for a mainframe. It connects to the communications lines on one end and the mainframe on the other. It transmits and receives messages, assembles and dissassembles packets and corrects errors.

FUD factor (**F**ear **U**ncertainty **D**oubt factor) Marketing strategy by a dominant or privileged organization that restrains competition by not revealing future plans.

full-duplex Transmitting and receiving simultaneously.

full featured Hardware or software that provides capabilities and functions comparable to the most advanced models or programs of that category.

full path Path name that includes the drive, starting or root directory, all attached subdirectories and ending with the file or object name.

full project life cycle Project from inception to completion.

full screen Programming capability that allows data to be displayed in any row or column on screen. Contrast with *teletype* mode.

fully populated Circuit board whose sockets are completely filled with chips.

function In programming, a software routine that does a particular task. When the program passes control to a function, it performs the task and returns control to the instruction following the calling instruction.

function keys Set of keyboard keys used to command the computer (labelled F1, F2, etc.). F1 is often the help key, but the purpose of any function key is determined by the software that is currently running.

functional specification Blueprint for the design of an information system. It provides documentation for the database, human and machine procedures, and all the input, processing and output detail for each data entry, query, update and report program in the system.

fuzzy computer Specially-designed computer that employs fuzzy logic and is used for AI applications.

fuzzy logic Mathematical technique that deals with values between 0 and 1 and is more analogous to human logic than digital logic. Results can be mostly true and mostly false rather than true and false.

fuzzy search Inexact search for data that finds answers that come close to the desired data. It can get results when the exact spelling is not known or help users obtain information that is loosely related to a topic.

G See *giga*.

game port I/O connector used to attach a joy stick. It is typically a 15-pin socket on the back of a PC.

gate Open/closed switch or a pattern of transistors that makes up a Boolean logic gate.

gated Switched "on" or capable of being switched on and off.

gateway Computer that interconnects and performs the protocol conversion between two types of networks. For example, a gateway between a personal computer LAN and a mainframe network. See *bridge*.

GB, Gb See *gigabyte* and *gigabit*.

Gbit See *gigabit*.

Gbits/sec (Giga**BITS** per **SEC**ond) Billion bits per second.

GBps, Gbps (Giga**B**ytes **P**er **S**econd, Giga**B**its **P**er **S**econd) Billion bytes per second. Billion bits per second.

GByte See *gigabyte*.

Gbytes/sec (Giga**BYTES** per **SEC**ond) Billion bytes per second.

GeoWorks Ensemble Popular graphical operating environment for DOS from GeoWorks, Inc., Berkeley, CA, that includes word processing, drawing, communications, card file and calendar applications. Users can launch all applications from within Ensemble.

ghost (1) Faint second image that appears close to the primary image on a display or printout.

(2) To display a menu option in a dimmed, fuzzy typeface, indicating it is not selectable at this time.

GHz (Giga**H**ert**Z**) One billion cycles per second.

GIF (**G**raphics **I**nterchange **F**ormat) Popular raster graphics file format developed by CompuServe that handles 8-bit color (256 colors) and achieves compression ratios of up to two to one.

giga Billion. Abreviated "G." It often refers to the precise value 1,073,741,824 since computer specifications are usually binary numbers.

gigabit One billion bits. Also Gb, Gbit and G-bit. See *giga* and *space/time*.

gigabyte One billion bytes. Also GB, Gbyte and G-byte. See *giga* and *space/time*.

gigaflops (**GIGA FL**oating point **OP**erations per **S**econd) One billion floating point operations per second.

GIGO (**G**arbage **In G**arbage **O**ut) "Bad input produces bad output." Data entry is critical. All possible tests should be made on data entered into a computer.
  GIGO also means "Garbage In, Gospel Out." People put too much faith in computer output!

GIS (**G**eographic **I**nformation **S**ystem) Digital mapping system used for exploration, demographics, dispatching and tracking.

glare filter Fine mesh screen that is placed over a CRT screen to reduce glare from overhead and ambient light.

glitch Temporary or random hardware malfunction.

global Pertaining to an entire file, database, volume, program or system.

goal seeking Ability to calculate a formula backward to obtain a desired input. For example, given the goal `gross margin = 50%` as well as the range of possible inputs, goal seeking attempts to obtain the optimum input.

gooey See *GUI*.

GPIB (**G**eneral **P**urpose **I**nterface **B**us) IEEE 488 standard parallel interface used for attaching sensors and programmable instruments to a computer. It uses a 24-pin connector. HP's version is the HPIB.

GPS (**G**lobal **P**ositioning **S**ystem) Series of continuously-transmitting satellites used for identifying earth locations. By triangulation from three satellites, a receiving unit can pinpoint where it is on earth.

GPSS (**G**eneral **P**urpose **S**imulation **S**ystem) Programming language for discrete event simulation, which is used to build models of operations such as manufacturing environments, communications systems and traffic patterns. Originally developed by IBM for mainframes, PC versions are available.

grabber hand Pointer in the shape of a hand that is moved by a mouse to "grab" and relocate objects on screen.

graceful degradation A system that continues to perform at some reduced level of performance after one of its components fails.

graceful exit Ability to get out of a problem situation in a program without having to turn the computer off.

grammar checker Software
that checks the grammar of a sentence.
It can check for and highlight
incomplete sentences, awkward phrases,
wordiness and poor grammar.

graphics Usually referred to as
"computer graphics," it is the creation of
pictures in the computer. See *raster
graphics, vector graphics, imaging, scanner,
digitizer tablet, drawing program, paint
program* and CAD.

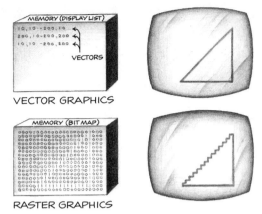

VECTOR GRAPHICS

RASTER GRAPHICS

graphics accelerator
High-performance video display board
that is optimized for graphical user
interfaces and performs several drawing
functions within the board's own
hardware. See *Winmark.*

graphics adapter Same as *video display board*

graphics card Same as *video display board.*

graphics engine Hardware that performs graphics processing independently of
the computer's CPU. It is typically designed for CAD systems and is more specialized
than a graphics accelerator.

graphics file File that contains only graphics data. Contrast with *text file* and
binary file.

graphics interface See *graphics language* and GUI.

graphics language High-level language
used to create graphics images. The language is
translated into images by software or specialized
hardware. See *graphics engine.*

graphics mode Screen mode that displays
only graphics. Contrast with *text mode.*

gray scale Series of shades from white to
black. The more shades, or levels, the more realistic
an image can be recorded and displayed, especially a
scanned photo. Scanners differentiate typically from
16 to 256 gray levels.

greek To display text in a representative form in
which the actual letters are not discernible, because
the screen resolution isn't high enough to display
them properly. Desktop publishing programs let you
set which font sizes should be greeked.

groupware Software that is designed for use in
a network and serve a group of users that work on a
related project.

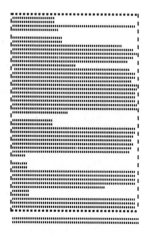

GREEKED PAGE OF TEXT

GUI (**G**raphical **U**ser **I**nterface) Graphics-based user interface that incorporates icons, pull-down menus and a mouse. Macintosh, Windows and Presentation Manager (OS/2) are examples.

GUI accelerator See *graphics accelerator*.

h (**H**exadecimal) Symbol that refers to a hex number. For example, 09h has a numeric value of 9, whereas 0Ah has a value of 10.

hacker Person who writes programs in assembly language or in system-level languages, such as C. Although it may refer to any programmer, it implies very tedious "hacking away" at the bits and bytes.

half-duplex Transmission of data in both directions, but only one direction at a time. Contrast with *full-duplex*.

half height drive 5.25" disk drive that takes up half the vertical space of first-generation drives. It is 1 5/8" high by 5.75" wide.

halftone In printing, the simulation of a continuous-tone image (shaded drawing, photograph) with dots. In photographically-generated halftones, a camera shoots the image through a halftone screen, creating smaller dots for lighter areas and larger dots for darker areas. Digitally-composed printing prints only one size of dot. In order to simulate varying-size dots, dithering is used, which creates clusters of dots in a "halftone cell."

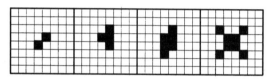

HALFTONE CELLS

handler Software routine that performs a particular task. For example, upon detection of an error, an error handler is called to recover from the error condition.

handset The part of the telephone that contains the speaker and the microphone.

handshaking Signals transmitted back and forth over a communications network that establish a valid connection between two stations.

Hardcard Family of hard disks from Plus Development Corp., Milpitas, CA, that house the disk drive and the control electronics together on an expansion board that plugs into a PC. It allows for a simpler installation and does not use up a drive bay. Many small, desktop computers have no spare drive bays.

hard disk Primary computer storage medium that is made of rigid disks with a magnetic recording surface. Personal computer hard disks hold from 20MB to over 1GB. Mini and mainframe hard disks can hold several gigabytes.

Fixed hard disks are permanently sealed in the drive. Removable hard disks are encased in disk pack or disk cartridge modules that can be moved between computers with the same kinds of drives.

Hard disks are usually low-level formatted from the factory, which records the original sector identification on them. See *floppy disk* and *format program*.

hard return Code entered into a text document by pressing the return (enter) key. DOS and OS/2 text files use a CR/LF (carriage return/line feed) pair, but this is not standard (WordPerfect uses only an LF). The Macintosh uses a CR and UNIX uses an LF.

hardware Machinery and equipment (CPU, disks, tapes, modem, cables, etc.). In operation, a computer is both hardware and software. One is useless without the other. The hardware design specifies the commands it can follow, and the instructions tell it what to do.

hardwired (1) Electronic circuitry that is designed to perform a specific task.

(2) Devices that are closely or tightly coupled. For example, a hardwired terminal is directly connected to a computer without going through a switched network.

Harvard Graphics Popular PC business graphics program from Software Publishing Corp., Mountain View, CA. It was one of the first business graphics packages and provides the ability to create columnar and free form text charts.

hash total Method for ensuring the accuracy of processed data. It is a total of several fields of data in a file, including fields not normally used in calculations, such as account number. At various stages in the processing, the hash total is recalculated and compared with the original. If any data has been lost or changed, a mismatch signals an error.

Hayes compatible Refers to modems controlled by the Hayes command language. See *AT command set*.

Hayes Smartmodem Family of intelligent modems for personal computers from Hayes Microcomputer Products, Inc., Atlanta, GA. Hayes developed the intelligent modem for first-generation personal computers in 1978, and its command language (Hayes Standard AT Command Set) for modem control has become an industry-standard.

HD (1) (**H**igh **D**ensity) Refers to 1.2MB 5.25" floppy disks and 1.44MB 3.5" floppy disks. See *high density*.

(2) (**H**ard **D**isk) For example, FD/HD refers to a floppy disk/hard disk device such as a controller.

HDX See *half-duplex*.

head See *read/write head*.

head crash Physical destruction of a hard disk. Misalignment or contamination with dust can cause the read/write head to collide with the disk's recording surface. The data is destroyed, and both the disk

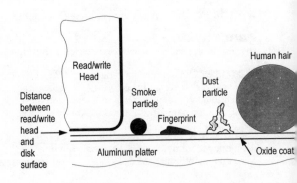

platter and head have to be replaced.

The read/write head touches the surface of a floppy disk, but on a hard disk, it hovers above its surface at a distance that is less than the diameter of a human hair.

header (1) In data processing, the first record in a file, used for identification. File name, date of last update and other status data are stored in it.

(2) In a document or report, common text printed at the top of every page.

(3) In communications, the first part of the message, which contains controlling data, such as originating and destination stations, message type and priority level.

(4) Any caption or description used as a headline.

help On-screen instruction regarding the use of a program. On PCs, pressing F1 is the de facto standard for getting help. With graphics-based interfaces (Mac, Windows, etc.), clicking a "?" or HELP button gets help. See *context sensitive help*.

Hercules Graphics De facto video display standard from Hercules Computer Technology Inc., Berkeley, CA, incorporated into all monochrome display boards for PCs. IBM's first monochrome display for the PC was text only. Hercules quickly developed a display adapter that combined graphics and text.

Hertz Frequency of electrical vibrations (cycles) per second. Abbreviated "Hz," one Hz is equal to one cycle per second. In 1883, Heinrich Hertz detected electromagnetic waves.

heterogeneous environment Equipment from a variety of manufacturers.

heuristic Method of problem solving using exploration and trial and error methods. Heuristic program design provides a framework for solving the problem in contrast with a fixed set of rules (algorithmic) that cannot vary.

Hewlett-Packard See *vendors*.

hex (**HEX**adecimal) Hexadecimal means 16. Base 16 numbering system used as a shorthand for representing binary numbers. Each half byte (four bits) is assigned a hex digit as follows:

Dec	Hex	Binary	Dec	Hex	Binary	Dec	Hex	Binary
0	0	0000	6	6	0110	10	A	1010
1	1	0001	7	7	0111	11	B	1011
2	2	0010	8	8	1000	12	C	1100
3	3	0011	9	9	1001	13	D	1101
4	4	0100				14	E	1110
5	5	0101				15	F	1111

hexadecimal See *hex*.

hi res Same as *high resolution*.

hidden file File classification that prevents a file from being accessed. It is usually an operating system file; however, utility programs let users hide files to prevent unauthorized access.

hierarchical Structure made up of different levels like a company organization chart. The higher levels have control or precedence over the lower levels. Hierarchical structures are a one to many relationship; each item having one or more items below it.

In communications, a hierarchical network refers to a single computer that has control over all the nodes connected to it.

hierarchical communications Network controlled by a host computer that is responsible for managing all connections. Contrast with *peer-to-peer communications*.

hierarchical file system File organization method that stores data in a top-to-bottom organization structure. All access to the data starts at the top (root directory in DOS and OS/2; the disk window in the Mac) and proceeds throughout the levels of the hierarchy.

high color Ability to generate 32,768 colors (15 bits) or 65,536 colors (16-bit). See *true color*.

high density Refers to increased storage capacity of bits and/or tracks per square inch. See *HD*.

high DOS memory Same as *UMA*.

high-level format Information (indexes, tables, etc.) recorded on a disk that is required by a specific operating system. See *low-level format*.

high-level language Machine-independent programming language, such as FORTRAN, COBOL, BASIC, Pascal and C. It lets the programmer concentrate on the logic of the problem to be solved rather than the intricacies of the machine architecture such as is required with low-level assembly languages.

high memory (1) Uppermost end of memory.

(2) In PCs, the area between 640K and 1M, or the 64K High Memory Area (HMA) area between 1024 and 1088K.

high resolution High-quality image on a display screen or printed form. The more dots used per square inch, the higher the quality. To display totally realistic images including the shades of human skin requires about 1,000x1,000 pixels on a 12" diagonal screen. Desktop laser printers print respectable text and graphics at 300 dpi, but typesetting machines print 1,270 and 2,540 dpi.

High Sierra First CD ROM standard named for an area near Lake Tahoe where it was conceived in 1985. Later evolved into the ISO 9660 standard.

high tech Refers to the latest advancements in computers and electronics as well as to the social and political environment and consequences created by such machines.

highlight To identify an area on screen in order to select, move, delete or change it in some manner.

highlight bar Currently-highlighted menu item. Choice is made by moving the bar to the desired item and pressing enter or clicking the mouse. The bar is a different color on color screens or reverse video on monochrome screens; for example, black on amber if normally amber on black.

HiJaak Graphics file conversion and screen capture program for PCs from Inset Systems Inc., Brookfield, CT. It supports a wide variety of raster and vector graphics formats as well as fax boards. It also handles conversion between PC and Mac formats.

HIMEM.SYS Extended memory (XMS) driver in DOS 5.0 and Windows 3.x that allows programs to cooperatively allocate extended memory in 286s and up.

hints Special additions to PostScript fonts that instruct the imaging device to alter space and other font features based on type size, especially for small font sizes.

HMA (**H**igh **M**emory **A**rea) In PCs, the first 64K of extended memory from 1024K to 1088K, which can be accessed by DOS in Real Mode. It is managed by the HIMEM.SYS driver.

Hollerith machine First automatic data processing system. It was used to count the 1890 U.S. census. Developed by Herman Hollerith, a statistician who had worked for the Census Bureau, the system used a hand punch to record the data in dollar-bill-sized punched cards and a tabulating machine to count them.

horizontal scan frequency Number of lines illuminated on a video screen in one second. For example, a resolution of 400 lines refreshed 60 times per second requires a scan rate of at least 24KHz. Contrast with *vertical scan frequency*.

host Main computer in a distributed processing environment. It typically refers to a large timesharing computer or a central computer that controls a network.

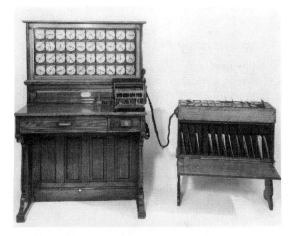

HOLLERITH CARD PUNCH, TABULATOR & SORT BOX
(Courtesy The Smithsonian Institution)

hotkey Key or key combination that causes some function to occur in the computer, no matter what else is currently running. It is commonly used to activate a memory resident (TSR) program.

hot link Predefined connection between programs so that when information in one database or file is changed, related information in other databases and files are also updated. See *compound document* and *OLE*.

hot spot Exact location of the screen cursor that points to and affects the screen object when the mouse is clicked. It is typically the tip of an arrow or finger pointer, but can be elsewhere with other cursor designs.

housekeeping Set of instructions that are executed at the beginning of a program. It sets all counters and flags to their starting values and generally readies the program for execution.

HP See *vendors*.

hub Central switching device for communications lines in a star topology. It may add nothing to the transmission (passive hub) or may contain electronics that regenerate signals to boost strengh as well monitor activity (active hub, intelligent hub).

HyperCard Application development system from Apple that runs on the Macintosh. Using visual tools, users build "stacks" of "cards" that hold data, text, graphics, sound and video with hypertext links between them. The HyperTalk programming language allows complex applications to be developed.

hypercube Parallel processing architecture made up of binary multiples of computers (4, 8, 16, etc.). The computers are interconnected so that data travel is kept to a minimum. For example, in two eight-node cubes, each node in one cube would be connected to the counterpart node in the other.

hypertext Linking related information. For example, by selecting a word in a sentence, information about that word is retrieved if it exists, or the next occurrence of the word is found. In the Windows and HyperCard versions of *Electronic Computer Glossary* (this book's big brother), you can click or highlight a computer term within the definition you're reading, and the definition for that term will be retrieved.

IBM See *vendors*.

IBM-compatible PC Personal computer that is compatible with the IBM PC and PS/2 standards.

IBM mainframes Large-scale computers from IBM. The following series all stem from the System/360 architecture introduced in 1964.

Date of Intro.	Series name and models
1964	System/360 (Models 20 thru 195)
1970	System/370 (Models 115 thru 168)
1977	303x series (3031, 3032, 3033)
1979	43xx series (4300 thru 4381, ES/4381)
1980	308x series (3081, 3083, 3084)
1986	3090 series (Models 120 thru 600, ES/3090)
1986	9370 series (Entry level; 9370, ES/9370)
1990	System/390 (ES/9000 Models 120 to 900)

IBM minicomputers Midrange computers from IBM. The following series comprise IBM's minicomputers over the years.

Date of Intro.	Series name	Date of Intro.	Series name
1969	System/3	1978	8100
1975	System/32	1983	System/36
1976	Series/1	1985	System/88
1977	System/34	1988	AS/400
1978	System/38		

IBM PC Personal computers from IBM. May refer to the first IBM personal computer model (the "PC") introduced in 1981, or generically to the entire PC, PS/1 and PS/2 line.

IC See *integrated circuit* and *information center*.

IC card See PC *card* and *memory card*.

icon Small, pictorial, on-screen representation of an object (file, program, disk, etc.) used in graphical interfaces. For example, to delete a file in the Macintosh, the icon of the file is dragged over to and placed on top of the icon of the wastebasket.

IDE (**I**ntegrated **D**rive **E**lectronics) Hard disk that contains a built-in controller. IDE-ready motherboards have a 40-pin socket that connects directly to an IDE drive eliminating the use of an expansion slot. In non-IDE-ready machines, the drive connects to an IDE host adapter that does plug into a slot.

if-then-else High-level programming language statement that compares two or more sets of data and tests the results.

image processing (1) Analysis of a picture using techniques that can identify shades, colors and relationships that cannot be perceived by the human eye. It is used to solve identification problems, such as in forensic medicine or in creating weather maps from satellite pictures and deals with images in raster graphics format that have been scanned in or captured with digital cameras.

(2) Image improvement, such as refining a picture in a paint program that has been scanned or entered from a video source.

(3) Same as *imaging*.

imagesetter See *phototypesetter*.

imaging Recording pictures into machine format: microfilm, videotape or computer. It refers to raster graphics formats generated by scanning or photographing pictures in · contrast to vector graphics generated in CAD and drawing programs. It also includes using OCR software to convert scanned text into machine code (ASCII, EBCDIC).

imaging model Set of rules for representing images.

impact printer Printer that uses a printing mechanism that bangs the character image into the ribbon and onto the paper. Line printers, dot matrix printers and daisy wheel printers are examples.

incremental backup Backing up only files that have been changed since the last backup, rather than backing up everything.

index In data management, the most common method for keeping track of data on a disk. Indexes are directory listings maintained by the operating system, DBMS or the application.

inference engine Processing program in an expert system. It derives a conclusion from the facts and rules contained in the knowledge base using various artificial intelligence techniques.

information Summarization of data. See *data*.

information appliance Type of future home or office device that can transmit to or plug into common public or private networks. Envisioned is a "digital highway," like telephone and electrical power networks.

information center Division within the company responsible for training users in computer applications and solving related personal computer problems.

information engineering Integrated set of methodologies and products used to guide and develop information processing within an organization. It starts with enterprise-wide stategic planning and ends with running applications.

information industry (1) Information publishing. Organizations that provide information via online services or through distribution by diskette or CD ROM.

(2) All computer, communications and electronics-related organizations, including hardware, software and services.

information management Discipline that analyzes information as an organizational resource. It covers the definitions, uses, value and distribution of all data and information within an organization whether processed by computer or not. See *data administration*.

information processing Same as *data processing*.

information resource management See *Information Systems* and *information management*.

information science Same as *information management*.

information service Any information retrieval, publishing, timesharing or BBS facility.

Information Services See *Information Systems*.

information system Business application of the computer. It is made up of the database, application programs, manual and machine procedures and encompasses the computer systems that do the processing. Following is how it fits into the world of computers.

STRUCTURE (is)   FUNCTION (does)

Management system
1. PEOPLE   Sets organization's goals and
2. MACHINES   objectives, strategies and tactics,
                       plans, schedules and controls

Information system
1. DATABASE   Defines data structures
2. APPLICATION   Data entry, updating,
   PROGRAMS   queries and reporting
3. PROCEDURES   Defines data flow

HOW SYSTEMS RELATE

Computer system
1. CPU   Processes (calculates, compares, copies)
2. PERIPHERALS   Store and retrieve
3. OPERATING   Manages the computer system
   SYSTEM

Information Systems Formal title for a systems/computer department. Other titles are Data Processing, Information Processing, Information Services, Management Information Systems, Management Information Services and Information Technology.

information warehouse Collection of all databases in an enterprise across all platforms and departments.

ink jet Printer mechanism that sprays one or more colors of ink onto paper and produces high-quality printing like that of a laser printer.

input device Peripheral device that generates input for the computer such as a keyboard, scanner, mouse or digitizer tablet.

input/output See I/O.

input program Same as *data entry program*.

install program Software that prepares a software package to run in the computer by copying the files from the distribution diskettes to the hard disk. It may decompress files and/or customize the new installation for the user's environment.

instruction Statement in a programming language or a machine instruction in machine language.

instruction set Repertoire of machine language instructions that a computer can follow (from a handful to several hundred). It is a major architectural component and is either built into the CPU or into microcode. Instructions are generally from one to four bytes long.

integer Whole number. An integer function would yield 123 from 123.898.

integrated circuit Formal name for chip.

integrated software package Several applications in one program, typically database management, word processing, spreadsheet, business graphics and communications. Framework, AppleWorks and Microsoft Works are examples.

Intel See *vendors*.

intelligence Processing capability. Every computer is intelligent!

intelligent modem Modem that not only converts signals but accepts and executes modem commands. See AT *command set*.

intelligent terminal Terminal with built-in processing capability, but no local disk or tape storage. Contrast with *dumb terminal*.

interactive Back-and-forth dialog between the user and a computer.

interactive cable TV Service in which viewers take part in TV programs by reacting to issues. A decoder and keyboard are required.

interactive session Back-and-forth dialogue between user and computer. Contrast with *batch session*.

interactive video Use of videodisc or CD ROM controlled by computer for an interactive education or entertainment program. See *videodisc* and CD ROM.

interface Connection and interaction between hardware, software and the user.

Hardware interfaces are the plugs, sockets and wires that carry electrical signals in a prescribed order. Software, or programming, interfaces (APIs) are the languages, codes and messages programs use to communicate between programs and to the hardware. User interfaces are the keyboards, mice, commands and menus used for communication between you and the computer.

interlaced Illuminating a CRT by displaying odd lines and then even lines (every other line first; then filling in the gaps). TV signals are interlaced (60 half frames/sec) as well as lower-cost high-resolution computer display systems. Interlacing uses half the signal information as non-interlacing and is less expensive to create.

TV's constant animation provides acceptable viewing, but flicker can be annoying on interlaced computer screens. Contrast with *non-interlaced*.

interleave See *sector interleave* and *memory interleaving*.

internal font Set of characters for a particular typeface that is built into a printer. Contrast with *font cartridge* and *soft font*.

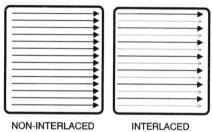

NON-INTERLACED   INTERLACED

internet (1) Large network made up of a number of smaller networks.

(2) (Internet) National research-oriented network comprised of over 3,000 government and academic networks in 40 countries.

Internet address Format for addressing a message to an Internet user. For example, the address of the Free Software Foundation is `gnu@prep.ai.mit.edu`, which means transmitting to the GNU mailbox via nodes PREP, AI and MIT. EDU is the domain, in this case "education."

internetwork To go between one network and another.

interoperable Ability for one system to communicate or work with another.

interpret To run a program one line at a time. Each line of source language is translated into machine language and then executed.

interpreter High-level programming language translator that translate and runs the program at the same time. It translates one program statement into machine language, executes it, then proceeds to the next statement.

RECORDS RECORDS RECORDS RECORDS RECORDS

interprocess communication See *IPC*.

interrecord gap Space generated between blocks of data on tape, created by the starting and stopping of the reel.

INTERRECORD
(INTERBLOCK) GAPS

interrupt Signal that gets the attention of the CPU and is usually generated when I/O is required. For example, hardware interrupts are generated when a key is pressed or when the mouse is moved. Software interrupts are generated by a program requiring disk input or output.

I/O (**I**nput/**O**utput) Transferring data between the CPU and a peripheral device. Every transfer is an output from one device and an input into another.

I/O bound Refers to an excessive amount of time getting data in and out of the computer in relation to the time it takes for processing it. Faster disk drives improve the performance of an I/O bound computer.

I/O card See *expansion board* and *PC card*.

I/O interface Channel, or pathway, between the CPU and a peripheral device. See *port* and *expansion slot*.

IPC (**I**nter**P**rocess **C**ommunication) Exchange of data between one program and another either within the same computer or over a network. It implies a protocol that guarantees a response to a request. Examples are OS/2's Named Pipes, Windows' DDE, Novell's SPX and Macintosh's IAC.

ips (**I**nches **P**er **S**econd) Measures the speed of tape passing by a read/write head or paper passing through a pen plotter.

IRMAboard Micro to mainframe board for PCs from DCA, Inc., Alpharetta, GA. It emulates the common IBM 3270 mainframe terminal allowing a PC access to centralized mainframe applications. IRMA is DCA's trade name for a variety of communications products. It is the lady's name, not an acronym.

ISA (**I**ndustry **S**tandard **A**rchitecture) Pronounced "i-suh." Refers to the original PC bus architecture, specifically the 16-bit AT bus. Contrast with *EISA* and *Micro Channel*.

ISAM (**I**ndexed **S**equential **A**ccess **M**ethod) Common disk access method that stores data sequentially, while maintaining an index of key fields to all the records in the file for direct access. The sequential order would be the one most commonly used for batch processing and printing (account number, name, etc.).

ISDN (**I**ntegrated **S**ervices **D**igital **N**etwork) International telecommunications standard for transmitting voice, video and data over a digital communications line. It uses out of band signalling, which provides a separate channel for control information.

ISO See *standards bodies*.

IT (**I**nformation **T**echnology) Same as *Information Systems*.

jaggies Stairstepped appearance of diagonal lines on a low-resolution graphics screen.

JCL (Job Control Language) Command language for mini and mainframe operating systems that launches applications. It specifies priority, program size and running sequence, as well as the files and databases used.

JEDEC & JEIDA See *standards bodies*.

jiff See GIF.

jitter Flickering transmission signal or display image.

LOW RESOLUTION
GRAPHICS

HIGH RESOLUTION
GRAPHICS

job Unit of work running in the computer. A job may be a single program or a group of programs that work together.

job stream Series of related programs that are run in a prescribed order. The output of one program is the input to the next program and so on.

join In relational database management, to match one file against another based on some condition creating a third file with data from the matching files. For example, a customer file can be joined with an order file creating a file of records for all customers who purchased a particular product.

Josephson junction Ultra-fast switching technology that uses superconductor materials, originally conceived by Brian Josephson. Circuits are immersed in liquid helium to obtain near-absolute zero degrees required for operation.

joy stick Pointing device used to move an object on screen in any direction. It employs a vertical rod mounted on a base that contains one or two buttons. It is used extensively in video games and in some CAD systems.

JPEG (Joint Photographic Experts Group) ISO/CCITT standard for compressing images using discrete cosine transform. It provides compression at variable ratios, providing 20 to 30:1 without noticeable loss. Ratios of 50:1 to 100:1 may be used if the loss in image can be tolerated (lossy compression).

jumper Metal bridge used to close a circuit. It can be a short length of wire or a plastic-covered metal block that is pushed onto two pins on a circuit board. It is often used in place of DIP switches.

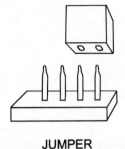

JUMPER

K See *kilo*.

KB, Kb See *kilobyte* and *kilobit*.

Kbit See *kilobit*.

Kbits/sec (**K**ilo**BITS** per **SEC**ond) Thousand bits per second.

KBps, Kbps (**K**ilo**B**ytes **P**er **S**econd, **K**ilo**B**its **P**er **S**econd) Thousand bytes per second. Thousand bits per second.

Kbyte See *kilobyte*.

Kbytes/sec (**K**ilo**BYTES** per **SEC**ond) Thousand bytes per second.

Kermit File transfer protocol developed at Columbia University, noted for its accuracy over noisy lines. Several extensions exist, including SuperKermit.

kernel Fundamental part of a program, such as an operating system, that resides in memory at all times.

key (1) Keyboard button.

(2) Data that identifies a record. Account number, product code and customer name are typical keys fields used to identify a record in a file or database. As an identifier, each key value must be unique in each record. See *sort key*.

(3) Numeric code used by an algorithm to create a code for encrypting data for security purposes.

key cap Replaceable, top part of a keyboard key. To identify commonly-used codes, it can be replaced with a custom-printed key cap.

key click Audible feedback provided when a key is pressed. It may be adjustable by the user.

key command Key combination (Alt-G, Ctrl-B, Command-M, etc.) used as a command to the computer.

key driven Any device that is activated by pressing keys.

key field See *key (2)*.

key word (1) Word used in a text search.

(2) Word in a text document that is used in an index to best describe the contents of the document.

(3) Reserved word in a programming or command language.

keyboard Set of input keys. On terminals and personal computers, it includes the standard typewriter keys and several specialized keys such as the Ctrl and Alt keys on the PC or Option and Apple keys on the Macintosh.

keyboard buffer Memory bank or reserved memory area that stores keystrokes until the program can accept them. It lets fast typists continue typing while the program catches up.

keyboard template Plastic card that fits over the function keys to identify each key's purpose in a particular software program.

keypad Small keyboard or supplementary keyboard keys; for example, the keys on a calculator or the number/cursor cluster on a computer keyboard.

keypunch To punch holes in a punched card. It is sometimes used to refer to typing on a computer keyboard.

KHz (KiloHertz) One thousand cycles per second. See *horizontal scan frequency*.

kilo Thousand. Abbreviated "K." It often refers to the precise value 1,024 since computer specifications are usually binary numbers. For example, 64K means 65,536 bytes when referring to memory or storage (64x1024), but a 64K salary means $64,000. The IEEE uses "K" for 1,024, and "k" for 1,000. See *binary values* and *space/time*.

kilobit One thousand bits. Also KB, Kb, Kbit and K-bit. See *kilo* and *space/time*.

kilobyte One thousand bytes. Also KB, Kbyte and K-byte. See *kilo* and *space/time*.

kiosk Small, self-standing structure such as a newstand or ticket booth. Unattended, multimedia kiosks dispense public information.

kludge Also spelled "kluge" and pronounced "klooj." A crude, inelegant system, component or program. It may refer to a makeshift, temporary solution to a problem as well as to any product that is poorly designed or that becomes unwieldy over time.

knowledge acquisition Process of acquiring knowledge from a human expert for an expert system, which must be carefully organized into IF-THEN rules or some other form of knowledge representation.

knowledge base Database of rules about a subject used in AI applications. See *expert system*.

knowledge based system AI application that uses a database of knowledge about a subject. See *expert system*.

knowledge domain Specific area of expertise of an expert system.

knowledge engineer Person who translates the knowledge of an expert into the knowledge base of an expert system.

knowledge representation Method used to code knowledge in an expert system, typically a series of IF-THEN rules (IF this condition occurs, THEN take this action).

L

label (1) In data management, a made-up name that is assigned to a file, field or other data structure.

(2) In spreadsheets, descriptive text that is entered into a cell.

(3) In programming, a made-up name used to identify a variable or a subroutine.

(4) In computer operations, a self-sticking form attached to the outside of a disk or tape in order to identify it.

(5) In magnetic tape files, a record used for identification at the beginning or end of the file.

LAN (**L**ocal **A**rea **N**etwork) Communications network that serves users within a confined geographical area. It is made up of file servers, which hold the programs and databases, and personal computers or workstations (clients), which perform the application processing. All stations in the network are connected via coaxial cable, twisted wire pair or optical fiber. Transmission between stations (nodes) is managed by a LAN access method, such as Ethernet or Token Ring, and the interaction between clients and servers is controlled by a network operating system, such as NetWare, LAN Manager or LANtastic. See *client/server, MAN* and *WAN*.

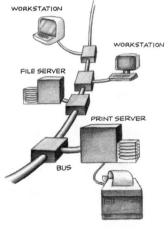

LOCAL AREA NETWORK

LAN administrator See *network administrator*.

LAN Manager LAN operating system from Microsoft that runs as an application under OS/2 in a server and supports both DOS, OS/2 and UNIX workstations.

Landmark rating Widely-used PC performance test from Landmark Research International, Clearwater, FL, that measures CPU, video and coprocessor speed. CPU speed is rated as the clock speed required in an AT-class machine that would provide equivalent performance.

landscape Printing orientation that prints data across the wider side of the form. Contrast with *portrait*.

LANtastic Popular peer-to-peer LAN operating system for PCs from Artisoft, Inc., Tucson, AZ, that is noted for its ease of use. It supports Ethernet, ARCNET and Token Ring as well as its own twisted-pair adapater at two Mbits/sec.

LapLink PC file transfer program from Traveling Software, Inc., Bothell, WA, that transfers data between laptops and desktop computers. LapLink Mac transfers files between PCs and Macs.

laptop computer Portable computer that has a flat screen and usually weighs less than a dozen pounds. It uses AC power and/or batteries. Most have connectors for an external monitor transforming them into desktop computers. See *notebook computer* and *pocket computer*.

laser (**L**ight **A**mplification from the **S**timulated **E**mission of **R**adiation) Device that generates a very uniform light (single wavelength) that can be precisely focused. It is used in a wide variety of applications, such as communications, printing and disk storage. It is used to transmit light pulses over optical fibers which, unlike electrical wires, are not affected by nearby electrical interferences.

laser printer Printer that uses the electrophotographic method used in copy machines to print a page at a time. A laser "paints" the dots of light onto a photographic drum or belt. The toner is applied to the drum or belt and then transferred onto the paper. Desktop printers use cut sheets like a copy machine. Large printers may use rolls of paper.

LaserJet Family of desktop laser printers from HP. Introduced in 1984 at $3,495, the first LaserJet revolutionized the desktop laser printer market. LaserJets print up to 600 dpi (LaserJet 4), although third-party enhancements increase resolution to 1200 dpi. PCL is the printer command language. Starting with the LaserJet III, Intellifont scalable fonts from Agfa CompuGraphic are also built in. See *WinJet*.

LaserWriter Family of 300 dpi desktop laser printers from Apple introduced in 1985. All models handle bitmapped fonts, and, except for the SC models, include PostScript and built-in AppleTalk connections.

latency Time between initiating a request for data and the beginning of the actual data transfer. On a disk, latency is the time it takes for the selected sector to come around and be positioned under the read/write head.

launch To cause a program to load and run.

layer (1) In computer graphics, one of several on-screen "drawing boards" for creating elements within a picture. Layers can be manipulated independently, and the sum of all layers make up the total image.

(2) In communications, a protocol that interacts with other protocols to provide all the necessary transmission services. See *OSI*.

LCD (**L**iquid **C**rystal **D**isplay) Display technology commonly used in digital watches and laptops. Because it uses less power, LCD replaced LED (light emitting diode) in digital watches years ago. Power is used only to move molecules rather than to energize a light-emitting substance.

leased line Private communications channel leased from a common carrier. It can be ordered in pairs, providing a four-wire channel for full-duplex transmission (dial-up system provides only two-wire lines). To improve line quality, it can also be conditioned.

Lempel Ziv Data compression algorithm that uses an adaptive compression technique (dynamically changes method based on the content of the data).

letter quality Print quality of an electric typewriter. Laser printers, ink jet printers and daisy wheel printers provide letter quality printing. 24-pin dot matrix printers provide near letter quality (NLQ), but the characters are not as dark and crisp.

librarian Person who works in the data library.

library (1) Collection of programs or data files.

(2) Collection of functions (subroutines) that are linked into the main program when it is compiled.

(3) See *data library*.

light pen Light-sensitive stylus wired to a video terminal used to draw pictures or select menu options. The user brings the pen to the desired point on screen and presses the pen button to make contact.

lightwave system Device that transmits light pulses over optical fibers at extremely high speeds (Gbits/sec range). Many intercity telephone trunks have been converted to lightwave systems.

LIGHT PEN

LIM EMS See *EMS*.

linear Sequential or having a graph that is a straight line.

linear programming Mathematical technique used to obtain an optimum solution in resource allocation problems, such as production planning.

line feed (1) Character code that advances the screen cursor or printer to the next line. The line feed is used as an end of line code in UNIX. In DOS and OS/2 text files, the return/line feed pair (ASCII 13 10) is the standard end of line code.

(2) Printer button that advances paper one line.

line frequency Number of times each second that a wave or some repeatable set of signals is transmitted over a line. See *horizontal scan frequency*.

line load (1) In communications, the percentage of time a communications channel is used.

(2) In electronics, the amount of current that is carried in a circuit.

line of code Statement in a source program. In assembly language, it usually generates one machine instruction, but in a high-level language, it may generate a series of instructions.

line printer Printer that prints one line at a time. Line printers are usually connected to mainframes and minicomputers.

line segment In vector graphics, same as *vector*.

line squeeze In a mail merge, the elimination of blank lines when printing names and addresses that contain no data in certain fields, such as title, company and second address line. See *field squeeze*.

link (1) In communications, a line, channel or circuit over which data is transmitted.

(2) In data management, a pointer embedded within a record that refers to data or the location of data in another record.

linked list In data management, a group of items, each of which points to the next item. It allows for the organization of a sequential set of data in noncontiguous storage locations.

Lisa First personal computer to include integrated software and use a graphical interface. Modeled after the Xerox Star and introduced in 1983 by Apple, it was ahead of its time, but never caught on due to its $10,000 price and slow speed.

LISP See *programming languages*.

list (1) Arranged set of data, often in row and column format.

(2) In fourth-generation languages, a command that displays or prints a group of selected records. For example, in dBASE, `list name address` displays all names and addresses in the current file.

LISA

load (1) To copy a program from some source, such as a disk or tape, into memory for execution.

(2) To fill up a disk with data or programs.

(3) To insert a disk or tape into a drive.

(4) In programming, to store data in a register.

(5) In performance measurement, the current use of a system as a percentage of total capacity.

(6) In electronics, the flow of current through a circuit.

load high In PCs, to load programs into high memory between 640KB and 1MB.

local bus In a PC, a data channel from the CPU to peripherals that runs at the higher CPU clock rate rather than the slower speeds of the ISA, EISA and Micro Channel buses. First implementations used proprietary designs; however, VESA has standardized the VL-bus, and Intel will introduce its PCI specification in 1993.

LocalTalk LAN access method from Apple that uses twisted pair wires and transmits at 230,400 bps. It runs under AppleTalk and uses a daisy chain topology that can connect up to 32 devices within a distance of 1,000 feet. Third party products allow it to hook up with bus, passive star and active star topologies.

log Record of computer activity used for statistical purposes as well as backup and recovery.

logic Sequence of operations performed by hardware or software. Hardware logic is made up of circuits that perform an operations. Software logic (program logic) is the sequence of instructions in a program.
    Note: Logic is not the same as logical. See *logical vs physical* and *Boolean logic*.

logical field Data field that contains a yes/no, true/false condition.

logical vs physical High-level versus low-level. Logical implies a higher view than the physical. For example, a message transmitted from Phoenix to Boston is logically going between the two cities; however, the physical circuit could be Phoenix to Chicago to Philadelphia to Boston.

login Same as *logon*.

Logo High-level programming language noted for its ease of use and graphics capabilities that stemmed from a National Science Foundation project. It contains many non-numeric programming functions found in LISP, but Logo's syntax is more understandable for novices.

logoff To quit, or sign off, a computer system.

logon To gain access, or sign in, to a computer system. If restricted, it requires users to identify themselves by entering an ID number and/or password. Service bureaus base their charges for the time between logon and logoff.

logout Same as *logoff*.

long-haul In communications, modems or communications devices that are capable of transmitting over long distances.

long lines In communications, circuits that are capable of handling transmissions over long distances.

loop In programming, a repetition within a program. Whenever a process must be repeated, a loop is set up to handle it. A program has a main loop and a series of minor loops, which are nested within the main loop. Learning how to set up loops is what programming technique is all about.

loosely coupled Refers to stand-alone computers connected via a network. Loosely coupled computers process on their own and exchange data on demand. Contrast with *tightly coupled*.

lossless compression Compression techniques that decompress data 100% back to original. Contrast with *lossy compression*.

lossy compression Compression techniques that do not decompress data 100% back to original. Images and audio samples may be able to afford small losses of resolution in order to increase compression. Contrast with *lossless compression*.

lost cluster Disk records that have lost their identification with a file name. This can happen if a file is not closed properly, which can sometimes occur if the computer is turned off without formally quitting an application.

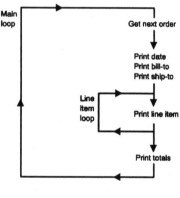

LOOP

The above example prints an invoice. The main loop reads the order record and prints the invoice until there are no more orders to read. After printing date and names and addresses, the program prints a variable number of line items. The code that prints the line items is contained in a loop and repeated as many times as required.

Lotus See *vendors*.

Lotus 1-2-3 Spreadsheet for PCs and a variety of computers from Lotus. Introduced in 1982, it was the first, new and innovative spreadsheet for the PC. Versions of Lotus are available for DOS, OS/2, Windows, Sun workstations, IBM mainframes, Digital's VAX minicomputer series and the Macintosh.

low-level format Sector identification recorded on a disk. Disks have two levels of formatting. The low-level format initiates the disk and creates the physical layout of the sectors required by the disk's controller. The high-level format lays out the indexes and tables used by the operating system to keep track of the data it writes into the sectors.

low-level language Programming language that is very close to machine language. All assembly languages are low-level languages. Contrast with *high-level language*.

low radiation Refers to video terminals that emit less VLF (Very Low Frequency) and ELF (Extremely Low Frequency) radiation. This level of radiation cannot be shielded by office partitions. It must be cancelled out from the CRT. Health studies on this are not conclusive and are very controversial. See *MPR II*.

low resolution Low-grade display or printing quality due to a lower number of dots or lines per inch.

lpi (**L**ines **P**er **I**nch) The number of lines printed in a vertical inch.

lpm (**L**ines **P**er **M**inute) Number of lines a printer can print or a scanner can scan in a minute.

LPT1 Logical name assigned to parallel port #1 in DOS and OS/2 (usually connected to a printer). A second parallel device is assigned LPT2. Contrast with *COM1*.

LQ See *letter quality*.

LU 6.2 SNA protocol that provides communications between two programs. It allows peer-to-peer communications as well as interaction between programs running in the host with PCs and other midrange computers. Also called APPC (Advanced Program to Program Communications).

M See *mega*.

Mac Same as *Macintosh*.

machine Any electronic or electromechanical unit of equipment. A machine is always hardware; however, "engine" refers to hardware or software.

machine dependent Refers to software that accesses specific hardware features and runs in only one kind of computer. Contrast with *machine independent*. See *device dependent*.

machine independent Refers to software that runs in a variety of computers. The hardware-specific instructions are in some other program (operating system, DBMS, etc.). Contrast with *machine dependent*. See *device independent*.

machine language Native langue of the computer. In order for a program to run, it must be in the machine language of the computer that is executing it. Although programmers may modify machine language in order to fix a running program, they do not create it. It is created by programs called *assemblers*, *compilers* and *interpreters*, which convert programming language into machine language.

Macintosh Series of personal computers from Apple introduced in 1984. It uses the Motorola 68000 processor family and a proprietary operating system that simulates a user's desktop on screen. This standard graphical user interface, combined with its built-in QuickDraw graphics language, has provided a measure of consistency and uniformity that is often copied, but still unmatched.

MAC II

In 1986, the Macintosh II was the first departure from the Mac's original hi-rise case and built-in small screen.

macro Series of menu selections, keystrokes and/or commands that have been recorded and assigned a name or key combination. When the name is called or the key is pressed, the macro is executed from beginning to end. See *batch file*.

macro recorder Program routine that converts menu selections and keystrokes into a macro. A user turns on the recorder, calls up a menu, selects a variety of options, turns the recorder off and assigns a key command to the macro. When the key command is pressed, the selections are executed.

magnetic disk Primary computer storage device that uses magnetic-coated disk platters divided into concentric tracks (circles within circles). Like magnetic tape, it can be re-recorded over and over. See *hard disk* and *floppy disk*.

magnetic stripe Small length of magnetic tape adhered to ledger cards, badges and credit cards. It is read by specialized readers that may be incorporated into accounting machines and terminals. Due to heavy wear, the data on the stripe is in a low-density format that may be duplicated several times.

magnetic tape Sequential storage medium used for data collection, backup and historical purposes. Like videotape, computer tape is made of flexible plastic with one side coated with a ferromagnetic material. Tapes come in reels, cartridges and cassettes of many sizes and shapes.

magneto-optic High-density, erasable recording method. Data is recorded magnetically like disks and tapes, but the bits are much smaller, because a laser is used to pinpoint the bit. The laser heats the bit to about 300 Celsius, at which temperature the bit is realigned when subjected to a magnetic field. In order to record new bits on the surface, existing bits have to be prealigned in one direction first. See *optical disk*.

mail merge Printing customized form letters. A common feature of a word processor, it uses a letter and a name and address list. In the letter, Dear A: Thank you for ordering B from our C store..., A, B and C are merge points into which data is inserted from the list. See *field squeeze* and *line squeeze*.

mainframe Large computer. In the "ancient" mid 1960s, all computers were called mainframes, since the term referred to the main cabinet that held the CPU. Today, it refers to a large computer system.

maintenance (1) Hardware maintenance is the testing and cleaning of equipment.

(2) Information system maintenance is the routine updating of master files; for example, adding and deleting employees and customers or changing credit limits and prices.

(3) Software or program maintenance is the updating of application programs in order to meet changing information requirements.

(4) Disk or file maintenance is the periodic reorganizing of online disk files that have undergone fragmentation due to continuous updating.

major key Primary key used to identify a record, such as account number or name.

MAN (**M**etropolitan **A**rea **N**etwork) Communications network that covers a geographic area such as a city or suburb. See *LAN* and *WAN*.

management science Study of statistical methods, such as linear programming and simulation, in order to analyze and solve organizational problems. Also called *operations research*.

management support See *DSS* and *EIS*.

map (1) Set of data that has a corresponding relationship to another set of data.

(2) List of data or objects as they are currently stored in memory or disk.

(3) To transfer a set of objects from one place to another. For example, program modules on disk are mapped into memory. A graphic image in memory is mapped onto the video screen. An address is mapped to another address.

mark sensing Detecting pencil lines in predefined boxes on paper forms or punched cards. The form is designed with boundaries for each pencil stroke that represents a yes, no, single digit or letter, providing all possible answers to each question.

mass storage High-capacity, external storage such as disk or tape.

massively parallel Parallel processing architecture that uses hundreds or thousands of processors.

master file Collection of records pertaining to one of the main subjects of an information system, such as customers, employees, products and vendors. Master files contain descriptive data, such as name and address, as well as summary information, such as amount due and year-to-date gross sales. Contrast with *transaction file*.

EMPLOYEE	Employee Number	Name	Address	Date of Hire	Date of Birth	Title	Job Class	Pay rate	YTD Gross
CUSTOMER	Customer Number	Name	Bill to	Ship to	Credit Limit	Date First Order	Sales to Date	YTD Sales	Balance Due
VENDOR	Vendor Number	Name	Address	Terms	Quality Rating	Shipping History			
PRODUCT	Product Number	Description	Quantity On hand	Location	Primary Vendor	Secondary Vendor			

TYPICAL MASTER RECORDS

master record Set of data for an individual subject, such as a customer, employee or vendor. See *master file*.

master-slave communications Communications in which one side, called the master, initiates and controls the session. The other side (slave) responds to the master's commands.

math coprocessor Mathematical circuit that performs high-speed floating point operations. It increases the performance of CAD applications, but the CAD program must activate its use. See *array processor* and *vector processor*.

matrix Array of elements in row and column form. See *x-y matrix*.

maximize In a graphical environment, to enlarge a window to full size. Contrast with *minimize*.

MB, Mb See *megabyte* and *megabit*.

Mbit See *megabit*.

Mbits/sec (Mega**BITS** per **SEC**ond) Million bits per second.

MBps, Mbps (Mega**B**ytes **P**er **S**econd, Mega**B**its **P**er **S**econd) Million bytes per second. Million bits per second.

Mbyte See *megabyte*.

Mbytes/sec (Mega**BYTES** per **SEC**ond) Million bytes per second.

MCA See *Micro Channel*.

MDA (**M**onochrome **D**isplay **A**dapter) First IBM PC monochrome video display standard for text only. Due to its lack of graphics, MDA cards were often replaced with Hercules cards, which provided both text and graphics.

media Material that stores or transmits data, for example, floppy disks, magnetic tape, coaxial cable and twisted wire pair.

media failure Condition of not being able to read from or write to a storage device, such as a disk or tape, due to a defect in the recording surface.

meg, mega (1) Million. Abreviated "M." It often refers to the precise value 1,048,576 since computer specifications are usually binary numbers. See *binary values* and *space/time*.

(2) (MEGA) Personal computer series from Atari that uses a Motorola 68000 CPU and includes the GEM interface, ROM-based TOS operating system, MIDI interface and a three-voice sound chip. It is ST compatible.

megabit One million bits. Also Mb, Mbit and M-bit. See *mega* and *space/time*.

megabyte One million bytes. Also MB, Mbyte and M-byte. See *mega* and *space/time*.

megaflops (mega **FL**oating point **OP**erations per **S**econd) One million floating point operations per second.

megahertz One million cycles per second. See *MHz*.

membrane keyboard Dust and dirtproof keyboard constructed of two thin plastic sheets (membranes) that contain flexible printed circuits made of electrically conductive ink. The top membrane is the printed keyboard and a spacer sheet with holes is in the middle. When a user presses a simulated key, the top membrane is pushed through the spacer hole and makes contact with the bottom membrane, completing the circuit.

memo field Data field that holds a variable amount of text. The text may be stored in a companion file, but it is treated as if it were part of the data record. For example, in the dBASE command `list name, biography`, name is in the data file (DBF file) and biography could be a memo field in the text file (DBT file).

memory (1) The computer's workspace (physically, a collection of RAM chips). It is an important resource, since it determines the size and number of programs that can be run at the same time, as well as the amount of data that can be processed instantly.

Memory is like an electronic checkerboard, with each square holding one byte of data or instruction. Each square has a separate address like a post office box and can be manipulated independently. As a result, the computer can break apart programs into instructions for execution and data records into fields for processing.

Other terms for memory are *RAM, main memory, main storage, primary storage, read/write memory, core* and *core storage*.

(2) Increasingly, the term is used to refer to disks as well as RAM memory. In the meantime, the use of the term for both working memory and permanent memory only adds confusion to an already-confusing industry. In this book, memory refers to RAM memory, and storage refers to disks and tapes.

memory allocation Reserving memory for specific purposes. Operating systems generally reserve all the memory they need at startup. Application programs take memory when loaded and may allocate more memory after being loaded. If there is not enough free memory, they cannot run.

memory bank (1) Physical section of memory. See *memory interleaving*.

(2) Refers generically to a computer system that holds data.

memory based Programs that hold all data in memory for processing. Almost all spreadsheets are memory based so that a change in data at one end of the spreadsheet can be instantly reflected at the other end.

memory cache See *cache*.

memory card (1) Credit-card-sized memory module used as a disk alternative in portable computers. Called IC cards, ROM cards and RAM cards, they use a variety of chip types, including RAM, ROM, EEPROM and flash memory. RAM cards use a battery to keep the cells charged. See *PC card* and "PCMCIA" under *standards bodies*.

(2) Printed circuit board that contains memory.

memory chip Chip that holds programs and data either temporarily (RAM), permanently (ROM, PROM) or permanently until changed (EPROM, EEPROM).

memory dump Display or printout of the contents of memory. When a program abends, a memory dump can be taken in order to examine the status of the program at the time of the crash.

memory interleaving Category of techniques for increasing memory speed. For example, with separate memory banks for odd and even addresses, the next byte of memory can be accessed while the current byte is being refreshed.

memory management Method used to control memory, which includes memory protection, virtual memory and bank switching techniques. With PCs, it refers to managing expanded and extended memory and the ability to load applications into the UMA (upper memory area). See *EMS*, *XMS* and *EMM*.

memory mapped I/O Peripheral device in which each element of its input or output is assigned to corresponding memory locations. For example, in a memory mapped display, each pixel or text character derives its data from a specific memory byte or bytes. The instant this memory is updated by software, the screen is displaying the new data.

memory protection Technique that prohibits one program from accidentally clobbering another active program. A protective boundary is created around the program, and instructions within the program are prohibited from referencing data outside of that boundary.

memory resident Program that remains in memory at all times. See *TSR*.

memory sniffing Coined by Data General, a diagnostic routine that tests the computer's memory constantly.

menu List of available options on screen. Selection is accomplished by highlighting the option with a mouse or cursor keys and clicking the mouse or pressing Enter.

menu bar Row of on-screen menu options.

menu-driven Using menus to command the computer. Contrast with *command-driven*.

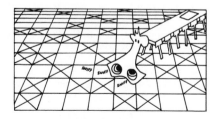

MEMORY SNIFFING

menuing software Software that provides a menu for launching applications and running operating system commands.

merge purge To merge two or more lists together and eliminate unwanted items. For example, a new name and address list can be added to an old list while deleting duplicate names or names that meet certain criteria.

message In communications, a set of data that is transmitted over a communications line. Just as a program becomes a job when it's running in the computer, data becomes a message when it's transmitted over a network.

message switch Computer used to switch data from one point to another. Computers have always been ideal message switches due to their input/output and compare capabilities. When a computer acts as a message switch, it inputs the message, compares its destination with a set of stored destinations and then outputs it to a selected communications channel.

metafile File that can define and store more than one type of information. For example, a Windows Metafile (WMF) can hold pictures in vector graphics and raster graphics formats as well as text.

Mflops See *megaflops*.

MFM (**M**odified **F**requency **M**odulation) Magnetic disk encoding method used on floppy disks and most hard disks under 40MB. It has twice the capacity of the earlier FM method, transfers data at 625 Kbytes per second and uses the ST506 interface.

MHz (**M**ega**H**ert**z**) One million cycles per second. Often references a computer's clock rate, which is a raw measure of its internal speed. For example, a 12MHz 286 computer processes data internally (calculates, compares, etc.) twice as fast as a 6MHz 286. However, disk speed and caching play a major role in the computer's actual performance.

MICR (**M**agnetic **I**nk **C**haracter **R**ecognition) Machine recognition of magnetically-charged characters typically found on bank checks and deposit slips. MICR readers detect the characters and convert them into digital code.

micro (1) Microcomputer or personal computer.

(2) One millionth. See *space/time*.

(3) Microscopic or tiny.

Micro Channel Also known as MCA (Micro Channel Architecture), it is an IBM 32-bit bus used in most PS/2s, the RS/6000 series and certain ES/9370 models. MCA boards can be designed for bus mastering and also contain built-in identification that eliminates manual settings often required with ISA boards. MCA boards are not interchangeable with ISA and EISA boards.

micro manager Person who manages personal computer operations within an organization and is responsible for the analysis, selection, installation, training and maintenance of personal computer hardware and software. See *information center*.

micro to mainframe Interconnection of personal computers to mainframes. See *3270*.

microchip Same as *chip*.

microcircuit Miniaturized, electronic circuit, such as is found on an integrated circuit. See *chip*.

microcomputer Same as *personal computer*.

microelectronics Miniaturization of electronic circuits. See *chip*.

microfloppy disk Floppy disk encased in a 3.5" wide, rigid plastic shell. Developed by Sony, it has become the medium of choice as it holds more data and is easier to handle than its 5.25" counterpart.

microprocessor CPU on a single chip. In order to function as a computer, it requires a power supply, clock and memory.

microsecond One millionth of a second. See *space/time*.

Microsoft See *vendors*.

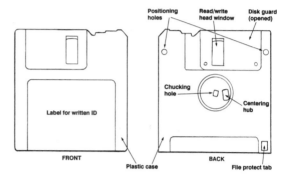

3.5" MICROFLOPPY DISK

Microsoft Word
Full-featured word processing program for PCs and the Macintosh from Microsoft. The DOS version provides both graphics-based and text-based interfaces for working with a document. Microsoft Word for Windows, often called Word for Windows (WinWord), is a separate and distinct product designed for the Windows interface.

Microsoft Works Integrated software package for PCs and the Macintosh from Microsoft. It provides file management with relational-like capabilities, word processing, spreadsheet, business graphics and communications capabilities in one package.

MIDI (**M**usical **I**nstrument **D**igital **I**nterface) Standard protocol for the interchange of musical information between musical instruments, synthesizers and computers. It defines the codes for a musical event, which includes the start of a note, its pitch, length, volume and musical attributes, such as vibrato. It also defines codes for various button, dial and pedal adjustments used on synthesizers. Because MIDI files contain descriptions of sounds, not the actual sounds, they take up considerably less space on a disk.

midrange computer Same as *minicomputer*, but excludes single-user minicomputer workstations.

millisecond One thousandth of a second. See *space/time*.

mini See *minicomputer*.

minicomputer Medium-scale computer that functions as a single workstation, or as a multiuser system with up to several hundred terminals. A system costs roughly from $20,000 to $250,000. Today, the term "midrange" is becoming popular for medium-sized computer. High-end microcomputers and low-end mainframes overlap in minicomputer price and performance.

minifloppy Floppy disk encased in a 5.25" wide, stiff plastic jacket. Introduced by Shugart in 1978, it superseded IBM's 8" floppy and has been used extensively ever since.

minimize In graphical environments, to reduce a window to an icon.

MIPS (**M**illion **I**nstructions **P**er **S**econd) Execution speed of a computer. For example, .5 MIPS is 500,000 instructions per second. High-speed personal computer and workstation CPUs perform in the 20-50 MIPS range. Digital's Alpha chip has a peak rate of 400 MIPS. Inexpensive microprocessors used in toys and games may be in the .05-.1 MIPS range.

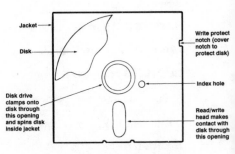

5.25" MINIFLOPPY DISK

mirroring See *disk mirroring*.

MIS (**M**anagement **I**nformation **S**ystem and **M**anagement **I**nformation **S**ervices) See *information system* and *Information Systems*.

mission critical Vital to the operation of an organization.

mixed object Same as *compound document*.

mnemonic Pronounced "nuh-monic." Means memory aid. A name assigned to a machine function. For example, in DOS, COM1 is the mnemonic assigned to serial port #1. Programming languages are almost entirely mnemonics.

MNP (**M**icrocom **N**etworking **P**rotocol) Family of communications protocols from Microcom, Inc., Norwood, MA, that have become de facto standards for error correction (classes 2 though 4) and data compression (class 5).

MO See *magneto-optic*.

mode Operational state that a system has been switched to. It implies at least two possible conditions. There are countless modes for hardware and software.

model (1) Style or type of hardware device.

(2) Mathematical representation of a device or process used for analysis and planning.

modem (**MO**dulator-**DEM**odulator) Device that adapts a terminal or computer to a telephone line. It converts the computer's digital pulses into audio frequencies and converts them back into pulses at the receiving side.

modular programming Breaking down the design of a program into individual components (modules) that can be programmed and tested independently. It is a requirement for effective development and maintenance of large programs and projects.

modulate To vary a carrier wave. Modulation blends a data signal (text, voice, etc.) into a carrier for transmission over a network. Major methods are AM (amplitude modulation) - modulate the height of the carrier wave, FM (frequency modulation) -

modulate the frequency of the wave, and PM (phase modulation) - modulate the polarity of the wave. Contrast with *demodulate*. See *carrier*.

module Self-contained hardware or software component that interacts with a larger system. Hardware modules are often made to plug into a main system. Program modules are designed to handle a specific task within a larger program.

monitor (1) Display screen used to present output from a computer, camera, VCR or other video generator. See *dot pitch, horizontal scan frequency* and *vertical scan frequency*.

(2) Software that provides utility and control functions such as setting communications parameters. It typically resides in a ROM chip and contains startup and diagnostic routines.

(3) Software that monitors the progress of activities within a computer system.

(4) Device that gathers performance statistics of a running system via direct attachment to the CPU's circuit boards.

monochrome Display of one foreground color and one background color; for example, black on white, white on black and green on black.

motherboard Main printed circuit board in an electronic device, which contains sockets that accept additional boards. In a personal computer, the motherboard contains the bus, CPU and coprocessor sockets, memory sockets, keyboard controller and supporting chips.
    Chips that control the video display, serial and parallel ports, mouse and disk drives may or may not be present on the motherboard. If not, they are independent controllers that are plugged into an expansion slot on the motherboard.

Motorola See *vendors*.

mouse Puck-like object used as a pointing and drawing device. As it is rolled across the desktop, the screen cursor (pointer) moves correspondingly.

mouse port Socket in the computer into which a mouse is plugged.

MPC (**M**ultimedia **PC**) Following are Microsoft's minimum requirements for a multimedia PC:

> 10Mhz 286 CPU, VGA display, 2MB RAM, 30MB hard disk, two-button mouse
> CD ROM with CD ROM extensions 2.2
> Sound card with 8-bit Linear PCM sampling, music synthesizer and analog mixing
> Serial, parallel, MIDI and joystick ports
> DOS 3.1, Windows 3.0 with multimedia extensions

MPR II Swedish government standard for maximum video terminal radiation. The earlier MPR I is less stringent.

ms See *millisecond*. Also see *vendors* (Microsoft).

MS-DOS (**M**icro**S**oft-**DOS**) Single user operating system for PCs from Microsoft. It is almost identical to IBM's DOS version, and both versions are called DOS generically.

MS-Windows (**M**icro**S**oft Windows) See *Windows*.

MTBF (**M**ean **T**ime **B**etween **F**ailure) Average time a component works without failure. It is the number of failures divided by the hours under observation.

Multifinder The part of the Macintosh operating system that manages the desktop and multiple applications on screen. First-generation Finder handles only one application at a time.

multifrequency monitor Monitor that adjusts to all frequencies within a range (multiscan) or to a set of specific frequencies, such as VGA and Super VGA.

multimedia Disseminating information in more than one form. Includes the use of text, audio, graphics, animated graphics and full-motion video. See MPC.

multiplexing Transmitting multiple signals over a single communications line or computer channel.

multiprocessing Simultaneous processing with two or more processors in one computer, or two or more computers processing together. When two or more computers are used, they are tied together with a high-speed channel and share the general workload between them. If one fails, the other takes over.

multiscan monitor Monitor that adjusts to all frequencies within a range. The multiscan monitor was popularized by NEC Technologies' MultiSync monitors. See *multifrequency monitor*.

multitasking Running two or more programs in one computer at the same time. It is controlled by the operating system. The number of programs that can be effectively multitasked depends on the amount of memory available, CPU speed, hard disk capacity and speed, as well as the efficiency of the operating system.

multithreading Multitasking within a single program. It is used to process multiple transactions or messages concurrently. It is also required for creating synchronized audio and video applications. Multithreading functions are often written in *reentrant code*.

multiuser Computer shared by two or more users.

MVS (**M**ultiple **V**irtual **S**torage) Introduced in 1974, the primary operating system used on IBM mainframes (the others are VM and DOS/VSE). MVS is a batch processing-oriented operating system that manages large amounts of memory and disk space. Online operations are provided with CICS, TSO and other system software.

naming service Software that converts a name into a physical address on a network, providing logical to physical conversion. Names can be user names, computers, printers, services or files.

nanosecond One billionth of a second. Used to measure the speed of logic and memory chips, a nanosecond can be visualized by converting it to distance. In one nanosecond, electricity travels about six inches in a wire. See *space/time.*

native mode In a computer capable of emulating one or more foreign computers, it is the primary running mode.

natural language English, Spanish, French, German, Japanese, Russian, etc.

NCR See *vendors.*

NCR paper (**N**o **C**arbon **R**equired paper) Multiple-part paper form that does not use carbon paper. The ink is adhered to the reverse side of the previous sheet.

NCSC (**N**ational **C**omputer **S**ecurity **C**enter) Arm of the U.S. National Security Agency that defines criteria for trusted computer products. Security levels are in its Orange Book (Trusted Computer Systems Evaluation Criteria, DOD Standard 5200.28). Level D is a non-secure system. Level C2 requires individual user logon with passwords and an audit mechanism. A1 is the highest level.

NetBIOS Commonly used transport protocol for PC local area networks introduced with IBM's PC Network and implemented in Microsoft's MS-Net and LAN Manager. Application programs use NetBIOS for client/server or peer-to-peer communications.

NetWare Family of popular network operating systems from Novell, Inc., Provo, UT, that runs on 286s and up and supports DOS, OS/2 and Mac workstations and a variety of LAN access methods, including Token Ring, Ethernet and ARCNET. It is the most widely-used network control program.

network In communications, the transmission channels and supporting hardware and software. See *LAN.*

network adapter Printed circuit board that plugs into a workstation or server and controls the exchange of data over a network. It performs the electronic functions of the access method (data link protocol), such as Ethernet, Token Ring and LocalTalk. The transmission medium (twisted pair, coax or fiber optic cable) physically interconnects all the adapters in the network.

network administrator Person who manages a communications network and is responsible for its efficient operation. Tasks include installing new applications and monitoring network activity.

network architecture (1) Design of a communications system, which includes the hardware, software, access methods and protocols used. It also defines the method of control: whether computers can act independently or are controlled by other computers monitoring the network. It determines future flexibility and connectability to foreign networks.

(2) Physical access method in a LAN, such as Ethernet, Token Ring and LocalTalk.

network card See *network adapter*.

network management Monitoring an active network in order to diagnose problems and gather statistics for administration and fine tuning.

network operating system Control program that resides in a file server in a LAN (NetWare, LANtastic, etc.). It handles the requests for data from the workstations in the network. In minis and mainframes, this category of software is called a *network control program* or *access method*. See VTAM.

network ready Software designed to run in a network. It implies that multiple users can share the databases without conflict.

network server See *file server*.

neural network Modeling technique based on the observed behavior of biological neurons and used to mimic the performance of a system. It consists of a set of elements that start out connected in a random pattern, and, based upon operational feedback, are molded into the pattern required to generate the required results. It is used in applications such as robotics, diagnosing, forecasting and pattern recognition.

NewWave PC operating environment from HP that runs between DOS and Windows. It integrates data using hot links and activates tasks using agents.

NeXT computers Family of UNIX-based workstations from NeXT, Inc., Redwood City, CA, that includes the NeXTstep user interface and provides high-resolution graphics and digital signal processing for CD-quality sound, image processing, data compression and voice recognition.

NeXTstep Graphical user interface and object-oriented development environment from NeXT Compuer. It allows for the creation of graphics-based, windows applications under UNIX.

NFS (Network File System) Distributed file system from SunSoft that allows data to be shared across a network regardless of machine, operating system, network architecture or protocol. This de facto UNIX standard lets remote files appear as if they were local on a user's machine.

nibble Half a byte (four bits).

NIC (Network Interface Card) Same as *network adapter*.

NiCad (Nickel CADmium) Material used for making rechargeable batteries. NiCad batteries have a memory. If recharged before completely drained, the next charge lasts only as long as the previous charge. For maximum storage capacity, a complete draining is periodically required. See *nickel hydride*.

nickel hydride Material used for making rechargeable batteries that provides more power per pound than NiCad batteries and does not exhibit the NiCad memory effect.

NIS (**N**etwork **I**nformation **S**ervices) Naming service from Sun that allows resources to be easily added, deleted or relocated. Formerly called Yellow Pages, NIS is a de facto UNIX standard. NIS+ is a redesigned NIS for Solaris 2.0.

node (1) In communications, a network junction or connection point (terminal or computer).

(2) In database management, an item of data that can be accessed by two or more routes.

(3) In computer graphics, an endpoint of a graphical element.

noise Extraneous signal that invades an electrical transmission. It can come from strong electrical or magnetic signals in nearby lines, from poorly fitting electrical contacts, and from power line spikes.

non-document mode Word processing mode used for creating source language programs, batch files and other text files that contain only text and no proprietary headers and format codes. All text editors, as well as XyWrite III Plus, automatically output this format.

non-impact printer Printer that prints without banging a ribbon onto paper, such as a thermal or ink jet printer.

non-interlaced Illuminating a CRT by displaying lines sequentially from top to bottom. Non-interlaced monitors eliminate annoying flicker found in interlaced monitors, which illuminate only half the screen at one time. See *interlaced* for an illustration.

non-numeric programming Programming that deals with objects, such as words, board game pieces and people, rather than numbers. Also called *list processing*.

non-preemptive multitasking Environment in which an application is able to give up control of the CPU to another application only at specific points in its running; for example, when it's ready to accept user input. One program can dominate a machine with this method. Contrast with *preemptive multitasking*.

non-procedural language Computer language that does not require traditional programming logic to be stated. For example, a command, such as LIST, might display all the records in a file on screen, separating fields with a blank space. In a procedural language, such as COBOL, all the logic for inputting each record, testing for end of file and formatting the screen has to be explicitly programmed.

Query languages, report writers, interactive database programs, spreadsheets and application generators provide non-procedural languages for user operation. Contrast with and see *procedural language* for a language example.

non trivial Favorite word among programmers for a difficult task.

non-volatile memory Memory that holds its content without power. Firmware chips (ROMs, PROMs, EPROMs, etc.) are examples. Disks and tapes may be called non-volatile memory, but they are usually considered storage devices.

Norton Utilities Disk management programs for the PC and Macintosh from Symantec Corp., Cupertino, CA. Includes programs to search and edit files, undelete files and restore damaged files among others. Originally from Peter Norton Computing, these programs were among the first to popularize disk utilities for the PC.

NOS See *network operating system.*

notebook computer Portable computer that typically weighs less than six pounds (heavier than a pocket computer; lighter than a laptop).

Novell network LAN controlled by one of Novell's NetWare operating systems. See *NetWare.*

NTSC (National TV Standards Committee) U.S. TV standard administered by the FCC that is currently 525 lines transmitted at 60 half frames/sec (interlaced). It is a composite of red, green and blue signals for color and includes an FM frequency for audio and an MTS signal for stereo. NTSC will reconvene when TV standards are changed.

NuBus Bus architecture (32-bit) originally developed at MIT and defined as a Eurocard (9U). Apple has changed its electrical and physical specifications for use in its Macintosh series. Many Macs have one or more NuBus slots for adding new peripheral devices.

null First character in ASCII and EBCDIC. In hex, it prints as 00; in decimal, it prints as a blank. It is naturally found in binary numbers when a byte contains no 1 bits. It is also used to pad fields and act as a delimiter; for example, in C, it specifies the end of a character string.

null modem cable RS-232-C cable used to connect two personal computers in close proximity. It connects to both serial ports and crosses the sending wire on one end to the receiving wire on the other.

number crunching Refers to computers running mathematical, scientific or CAD applications, which perform large amounts of calculations.

numerical control Category of automated machine tools, such as drills and lathes, that operate from instructions in a program. Numerical control (NC) machines are used in manufacturing tasks, such as milling, turning, punching and drilling.

OA See *office automation.*

object (1) In object-oriented programming, a self-contained module of data and its associated processing.

(2) In a compound document, an independent block of data, text or graphics that was created by a separate application.

object code Same as *machine language.*

object computer Same as *target computer.*

object language Same as *target language.*

object-oriented programming Abbreviated "OOP," a programming technology that is more flexible than standard programming. It is an evolutionary form of modular programming with formal rules that allow pieces of software to be reused and interchanged between programs more easily.

It deals with self-contained modules, or objects, that hold both the data and the routines that act upon the data. This is called *encapsulation* and these user-defined data types are called *classes.* One instance of a class is the *object.*

Another major feature is *inheritance.* Classes are created in hierarchies that allow the knowledge in one class to pass down the hierarchy. The object MACINTOSH could be one instance of a PERSONAL COMPUTER class and inherit all the properties associated with it.

Xerox's Smalltalk was the first object-oriented language. Today, C++ is the popular OOP language because it is an extension of traditional C. See *programming languages.*

object-oriented technology Variety of disciplines that support object-oriented programming (OOP), including object-oriented analysis and object-oriented design (OOA, OOD).

object program Machine language program ready to run.

OCR (**O**ptical **C**haracter **R**ecognition) Machine recognition of printed characters. OCR systems can recognize many different OCR fonts, as well as typewriter and computer-printed characters. Advanced OCR systems can recognize hand printing.

OEM (**O**riginal **E**quipment **M**anufacturer) Manufacturer that sells equipment to a reseller. Also refers to the reseller itself. OEM customers either add value to the product before reselling it, private label it, or bundle it with their own products. See *VAR.*

office automation Integration of office information functions, including word processing, data processing, graphics, desktop publishing and e-mail.

offline Not connected to or not installed in the computer. If a terminal, printer or other device is physically connected to the computer, but is not turned on or in ready mode, it is still considered offline. Contrast with *online*.

offline storage Disks and tapes that are kept in a data library.

offload To remove work from one computer and do it on another. See *cooperative processing*.

offset (1) Distance from a starting point, either the start of a file or the start of a memory address.

(2) In word processing, the amount of space a document is printed from the left margin.

OLE (**O**bject **L**inking and **E**mbedding) Windows compound document protocol. The "client" application creates the document; the "server" application creates an object within the document. When a user double clicks on an embedded object in a client application, the server application is loaded and the appropriate data file is retrieved.

online (1) Peripheral device (terminal, printer, etc.) that is ready to operate. A printer can be attached and turned on, yet still not online, if the ONLINE or SEL light is out. Pressing the ONLINE button will usually turn it back online.

(2) An online computer system refers to a system with terminals, but does not imply how the system operates. All the following are online systems: Data collection systems accept data from terminals, but do not update master files. Interactive systems imply data entry and updating. Transaction processing systems update master files as soon as the transactions arrive. Realtime systems provide an immediate response to a question.

Want to impress your friends?

Complete overkill, but not incorrect to say that one has an online, realtime, interactive, transaction processing system. However, don't say this to an experienced systems analyst!

online help On-screen instruction that is immediately available.

online industry Collection of organizations that provide dial-up access to e-mail and database services.

online services Following are major online information service organizations, including the types of databases provided. "Wide variety" generally includes news, weather and shopping as well as information on a host of topics. Many services provide e-mail.

America Online, Inc.
Databases: wide variety, personal computer, technical
  8619 Westwood Center Dr., Vienna, VA 22182, 800/827-6364, 703/448-8700

BIX
Databases: personal computer technical
  Byte Information Exchange, General Videotex Corp., 1030 Massachusetts Ave.
  Cambridge, MA 02138, 800/695-4775, 617/491-3393

CompuServe Information Service, Inc.
Databases: wide variety, personal computer, technical
  P.O. Box 20212, Columbus, OH 43220, 800/848-8199 (Ohio)
  800/848-8990, 614/457-8650

DataTimes Corporation
Databases: newspapers, magazines, financial
14000 Quail Springs Pkwy., Oklahoma City, OK 73134, 800/642-2525, 405/751-6400

DELPHI
Databases: wide variety, access to DIALOG
General Videotex Corp., 1030 Massachusetts Ave., Cambridge, MA 02138
800/544-4005, 617/491-3393

DIALOG Information Services, Inc.
Databases: over 400 (largest)
3460 Hillview Avenue, Palo Alto, CA 94304, 800/334-2564, 415/858-2700

Dow Jones News/Retrieval Service
Databases: financial plus shopping airline reservations, etc.
P.O. Box 300, Princeton, NJ 08543, 800/522-3567, 609/520-4000

EasyLink
Services: e-mail, Telex, EDI
Databases: access to major providers (DIALOG, CompuServe, etc.)
AT&T EasyLink Services, 400 Interpace Pkwy., Parsippany, NJ 07054
800/242-6005, 201/331-4000

GEnie
Databases: wide variety
General Electric Information Services Co., 401 N. Washington St.
Rockville, MD 20850, 800/638-9636, 301/340-4000

Mead Data Central
Databases: news (NEXIS), legal (LEXIS)
P.O. Box 933, Dayton, OH 45401, 800/227-4908, 513/865-6800

Maxwell Online
Databases: medical (BRS), patent, trademark (ORBIT)
8000 Westpark Dr., McClean, VA 22102, ORBIT 800/456-7248, BRS 800/289-4277

MEDLARS
Databases: medical
National Library of Medicine, 8600 Rockville Pike, Bethesda, MD 20894
800/638-8480, 301/496-6193

MCI Mail
Services: e-mail, Telex, fax
Databases: access to Dow Jones
1133 19th St., NW, Washington, DC 20036, 800/444-6245, 202/833-8484

National Videotex Network
Databases: wide variety
5555 San Felipe, Suite 1200, Houston, TX 77056, 800/336-9096, 713/877-4444

NewsNet, Inc.
Databases: newsletters
945 Haverford Rd., Bryn Mawr, PA 19010, 800/952-0122, 215/527-8030

PRODIGY
Databases: wide variety, shopping
  445 Hamilton Ave., White Plains, NY 10601, 800/776-3449, 914/993-8848

VU/TEXT Information Services, Inc.
Databases: newspapers
  325 Chestnut St., Suite 1300, Philadelphia, PA 19106, 800/323-2940, 215/574-4400

WESTLAW
Databases: legal (plus access to DIALOG and Dow Jones)
  West Publishing Co., 610 Opperman Dr., St. Paul, MN 55123, 800/WESTLAW
  612/687-7000

ZiffNet
Databases: PCs (downloads, technical info.)
  25 First St., Cambridge, MA 02141, 800/666-0330, 617/252-5000

OOP See *object-oriented programming.*

open (1) To identify a disk or tape file for reading and writing. The open procedure "locks on" to an existing file or creates a new one.

(2) With regard to a switch, open is "off."

open architecture System in which the specifications are made public in order to encourage third-party vendors to develop add-on products. Much of Apple's early success was due to the Apple II's open architecture. The PC is open architecture.

open system Vendor-independent system that is designed to interconnect with a variety of products. It implies that standards are determined from a consensus of interested parties rather than one or two vendors. Contrast with *closed system.*

operating system Master control program that runs the computer. It is the first program loaded when the computer is turned on, and its main part, called the *kernel*, resides in memory at all times. It may be developed by the vendor of the computer it's running in or by a third party.
    It is an important component of the computer system, because it sets the standards for the application programs that run in it. All programs must "talk to" the operating system. Also called an *executive* or *supervisor.*

optical disk Direct access disk written and read by light. Music CDs, CD ROMs and videodiscs are optical disks recorded at the time of manufacture and cannot be erased. WORM disks are recorded in the user's environment, but cannot be erased.
    Erasable optical disks function like magnetic disks and can be rewritten over and over. In the late 1980s, a variety of erasable optical disks were introduced that use magneto-optic, dye polymer and phase change recording technologies.

optical fiber Thin glass wire designed for light transmission, capable of transmitting billions of bits per second. Unlike electrical pulses, light pulses are not affected by random radiation in the environment.

OS See *operating system.*

OS/2 Single user, multitasking PC operating system with a graphical interface (Presentation Manager) similar to Windows. Early versions were developed jointly by Microsoft and IBM for 286s and up (16 bit). New versions (32-bit) for 386s and up are developed independently. IBM's OS/2 Version 2.0 runs OS/2, DOS and Windows programs. Microsoft's version is Windows NT.

OSF (**O**pen **S**oftware **F**oundation) Non-profit organization dedicated to delivering an open computing environment. Major OSF standards are the OSF/1 operating system (version of UNIX), the Motif graphical user interface, the Distributed Computing Environment (DCE) and the Distributed Management Environment (DME) protocols.

OSI (**O**pen **S**ystem **I**nterconnection) ISO standard for worldwide communications that defines a framework for implementing protocols in seven layers. It is similar to IBM's SNA layers, but not identical. Control is passed from one layer to the next, starting at the application layer in one station, proceeding to the bottom layer, over the channel to the next station and back up the hierarchy. Most vendors have agreed to support OSI in one form or another. OSI requires more detailed specifications and enormous cooperation to make it a universal standard like the telephone system.

The first two layers are commonly used in personal computer communications (Xmodem, Zmodem, Ethernet, Token Ring). See *communications protocol* and chart below.

outline font Type of font made from basic outlines of each character. The outlines are scaled into actual characters (bitmaps) before printing. See *scalable font.*

output (1) Any computer-generated information displayed on screen, printed on paper or in machine readable form, such as disk and tape.

(2) To transfer or transmit from the computer to a peripheral device or communications line.

output device
Any peripheral that presents output from the computer, such as a screen or printer. Although disks and tapes receive output, they are called storage devices.

outsourcing
Contracting with outside consultants, software houses or service bureaus to perform systems analysis, programming and datacenter operations. See *facilities management.*

OverDrive Intel's 486 upgrade CPUs. See *486.*

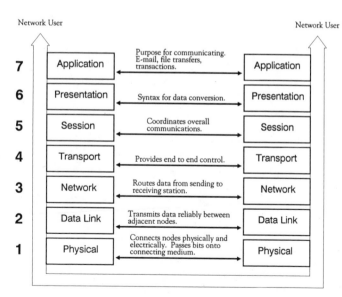

OSI LAYERS

overflow error Error that occurs when calculated data cannot fit within the designated field. The result field is usually left blank or is filled with some symbol to flag the error condition.

overhead (1) Amount of processing time used by system software, such as the operating system, TP monitor or database manager.

(2) In communications, the additional codes transmitted for control and error checking purposes.

overlay (1) Preprinted, precut form placed over a screen, key or tablet for indentification purposes. See *keyboard template*.

(2) Program segment called into memory when required. When a program is larger than the memory capacity of the machine, the parts of the program that are not in constant use can be set up as overlays.

overlay card Controller that digitizes NTSC signals from a video source for display in the computer.

P

pack (1) To compress data in order to save space. Unpack refers to decompressing data. See *data compression*.

(2) In database programs, a command that removes records that have been marked for deletion.

packet switching Technique for handling high-volume traffic in a network by breaking apart messages into fixed length packets that are transmitted to their destination through the most expedient route. All packets in a single message may not travel the same route (dynamic routing). The destination computer reassembles the packets into their proper sequence.

page break In printing, a code that marks the end of a page. A "hard" page break, inserted by the user, breaks the page at that location. "Soft" page breaks are created by word processing and report programs based on the current page length setting.

page description language Device-independent, high-level language for defining printer output. If an application generates output in a page description language, such as PostScript, the output can be printed on any printer that supports it.

page recognition Software that recognizes the content of a printed page which has been scanned into the computer. It uses OCR to convert the printed words into computer text and should be able to differentiate text from other elements on the page, such as pictures and captions.

PageMaker Full-featured desktop publishing program for the PC and Macintosh from Aldus Corp., Seattle, WA. Originally introduced for the Mac in 1985, it helped sell plenty of Macintoshes and set the standard for desktop publishing. In fact, Paul Brainerd, president of Aldus, coined the term "desktop publishing." The PC version was introduced in 1987.

paint (1) In computer graphics, to "paint" the screen using a tablet stylus or mouse to simulate a paintbrush.

(2) To transfer a dot matrix image as in the phrase "the laser printer paints the image onto a photosensitive drum."

(3) To create a screen form by typing anywhere on screen. To "paint" the screen with text.

paint program Graphics program that allows the user to simulate painting on screen with the use of a graphics tablet or mouse. Paint programs create raster graphics images.

palette (1) In computer graphics, the total range of colors that can be used for display, although typically only a subset of them can be used at one time. May also refer to the collection of painting tools available to the user.

(2) Set of functions or modes.

palmtop Computer small enough to hold in one hand and operate with the other. Palmtops may have specialized keyboards or keypads for data entry applications or have small qwerty keyboards.

pan (1) In computer graphics, to move (while viewing) to a different part of an image without changing magnification.

(2) To move (while viewing) horizontally across a text record.

paper tape (1) Early form of data storage that held patterns of punched holes.

(2) Paper roll printed by a calculator or cash register.

Paradox Network-ready relational DBMS for PCs from Borland that is known for its ease of use and query by example method for asking questions. Its PAL programming language allows for the development of complete business applications.

parallel port I/O attachment used to hook up a printer or other parallel interface device. On a PC, it is a 25-pin female DB-25 connector. See *printer cable*.

parallel processing (1) Architecture within a single computer that performs more than one operation at the same time. See *pipeline processing* and *vector processor*.

(2) Multiprocessing architecture made up of multiple CPUs or computer systems. Either one operation is performed on many sets of data, or different parts of the job are worked on simultaneously. See *hypercube*.

parallel transmission Transmitting data over multiple lines, one or more bytes at a time. Contrast with *serial transmission*.

parameter Any value passed to a program or routine in order to modify it. Software is sometimes written to accept optional directions, which are entered on the command line with the program name when the program is loaded. Examples are file names, coordinates, specific codes, etc. See *switch*.

PARC (**P**alo **A**lto **R**esearch **C**enter) Xerox's research and development center where the Smalltalk programming language and GUI interface were developed. Established in 1970, it is in the Stanford University Industrial Park in Palo Alto, CA.

parent-child In database management, a relationship between two files. The parent file contains required data about a subject (customers, vendors, etc.). The child is the offspring (orders, purchases, etc.).

parent program Main, or primary, program or first program loaded into memory. See *child program*.

parity bit Extra bit attached to the byte, character or word used to detect errors in transmission.

parity checking Error detection technique that tests the integrity of digital data within the computer system or over a

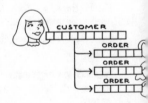

PARENT-CHILD

network. Parity checking uses an extra ninth bit that holds a 0 or 1 depending on the data content of the byte. Each time a byte is transferred or transmitted, the parity bit is tested.

park To retract the read/write head on a hard disk to its home location before the unit is physically moved in order to prevent damage. Most modern drives park themselves when the power is turned off.

parse To analyze a sentence or language statement. Parsing breaks down words into functional units that can be converted into machine language. For example, to parse the dBASE expression **sum salary for title = "MANAGER"**, SUM must be identified as the primary command, FOR as a conditional search, TITLE as a field name and MANAGER as the data to be searched.

parser Routine that performs parsing operations on a computer or natural language.

partition Reserved part of disk or memory that is set aside for some purpose.

Pascal See *programming languages*.

passive matrix LCD Common LCD technology that illuminates a pixel by sending current down the appropriate row and column. Contrast with *active matrix* LCD.

password Word or code used to serve as a security measure against unauthorized access to data. It is normally managed by the operating system or DBMS. However, the computer can only verify the legitimacy of the password, not the legitimacy of the user.

patch Temporary or quick fix to a program. Too many patches in a program make it difficult to maintain. It may also refer to changing the actual machine code when it is inconvenient to recompile the source program.

path (1) In communications, the route between any two nodes.

(2) In database management, the route from one set of data to another; for example, from customers to orders.

(3) Identifiable route to a file on a disk. For example, the MYLIFE file in the subdirectory STORIES in the directory JOE would look like **c:\joe\stories\mylife** in DOS, **/joe/stories/mylife** in UNIX and **hard disk:joe:stories:mylife** in the Macintosh, assuming "hard disk" as the disk name (sometimes command line path names are used in the Mac).

PBX (**P**rivate **B**ranch e**X**change) Inhouse telephone switching system that interconnects telephone extensions to each other, as well as to the outside telephone network. It may include functions such as least cost routing for outside calls, call forwarding, conference calling and call accounting.

Modern PBXs use all-digital methods for switching and can often handle digital terminals and telephones along with analog telephones.

PC (1) (**P**ersonal **C**omputer) Machines that conform to the PC standard, originally developed by IBM and subsequently governed by Intel, Microsoft and major PC vendors collectively. The PC is the world's largest computer base; 1993 estimates are 100 million units worldwide.

(2) (**P**ersonal **C**omputer) Any personal computer.

(3) Sometimes refers to first-generation IBM models PC, XT and AT in contrast with second-generation PS/2s.

(4) See *printed circuit board.*

PC bus Bus architecture used in first-generation IBM PCs. It refers to the original 8-bit bus and the 16-bit extension introduced with the AT. 8-bit boards fit in 8-bit and 16-bit slots, but 16-bit boards fit only in a 16-bit slot. Also called *ISA* bus. Contrast with *EISA* and *Micro Channel.*

PC card (1) Memory card, I/O card or memory and I/O card. The "PC Card" logo refers to PCMCIA Version 2.0 and JEIDA Version 4.1, compatible standards as of late 1991. See *standards bodies.*

(2) Expansion board for a PC.

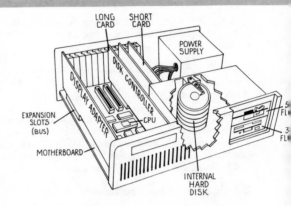

INTERNAL LAYOUT OF A PC

PC-DOS DOS operating system from Microsoft supplied by IBM for its personal computers. PC-DOS and MS-DOS are almost identical, and both are simply called DOS.

PC network (1) Network of IBM and/or IBM-compatible PCs.

(2) Network of any variety of personal computers.

(3) (PC Network) First PC LAN from IBM introduced in 1984. It used the CSMA/CD access method and introduced the NetBIOS interface. Token Ring Network support was later added. Microsoft's version was called MS-Net.

PC Paintbrush PC paint program from ZSoft Corp., Marietta, GA, that set a defacto standard graphics format. Its PCX raster graphics format handles monochrome, 2-bit, 4-bit, 8-bit and 24-bit color.

PC Tools Deluxe Comprehensive package of PC utilities from Central Point Software, Beaverton, OR, that includes a DOS shell as well as file management, communications, disk caching, backup and data compression utilities.

PCL (**P**rinter **C**ontrol **L**anguage) Command language for the HP LaserJet printers. It has become a de facto standard used in many printers and typesetters. PCL Level 5, introduced with the LaserJet III in 1990, also supports Compugraphic's Intellifont scalable fonts.

PCM (1) (**P**ulse **C**ode **M**odulation) Technique for digitizing speech by sampling the sound waves and converting each sample into a binary number. It uses waveform coding that samples a 4KHz bandwidth 8,000 times a second. Each sample is an 8 bit number, resulting in 64K bits of data per second.

(2) (**P**lug **C**ompatible **M**anufacturer) Organization that makes a computer or electronic device that is compatible with an existing machine.

PCMCIA See *standards bodies.*

PCX See *PC Paintbrush.*

PD software See *public domain software*.

PDA (**P**ersonal **D**igital **A**ssistant) Handheld computer that serves an an organizer, electronic book or note taker and includes features such as pen-based entry and wireless transmission to a cellular service or desktop system.

peer-to-peer communications Communications in which both sides have equal responsibility for initiating the session. Contrast with *master-slave communications*.

peer-to-peer network Local area network that allows all users access to data on all workstations. Dedicated file servers are not required, but may be used.

pel Same as *pixel*.

pen-based Using a stylus to enter hand writing and marks into a computer.

Pentium Successor to the 486 CPU from Intel. Originally called the 586 and code named "P5," the Pentium is at least twice as fast as a 486. See *x86*.

peripheral Any hardware device connected to a computer, such as a monitor, keyboard, printer, plotter, disk, tape, graphics tablet, scanner, joy stick, paddle or mouse.

personal computer Computer that serves one user. Same as *microcomputer*.

phototypesetter Device that creates professional-quality text. Input comes from the keyboard, disk, tape or modem. Its output is a paper-like or transparent film that is processed into a camera-ready master for printing. Phototypesetters that handle graphics as well as text are called *imagesetters*.

picture In programming, a mask, or pattern, that shows how data will be displayed or printed. (999) 999-9999 is a typical picture for a telephone number.

THE FIRST PERSONAL COMPUTER
(Courtesy Xerox Corporation)
In the mid 1970s, Xerox developed the Alto, forerunner of its Star workstation and inspiration for Apple's Lisa and Macintosh.

pie chart Graphical representation of information in which each unit of data is represented as a pie-shaped piece of a circle. See *business graphics*.

PIF (**P**rogram **I**nformation **F**ile) Windows data file used to hold requirements for DOS applications running under Windows. Windows comes with a variety of PIFs, but users can edit them and new ones can be created with the PIF editor if a DOS application doesn't work properly. An application can be launched by clicking on its PIF.

piggyback board Small printed circuit board that plugs into another circuit board in order to enhance its capabilities. It does not plug into the motherboard, but would plug into the boards that plug into the motherboard.

PIM (**P**ersonal **I**nformation **M**anager) Combination word processor, database and desktop accessory program. It allows the user to tie together more loosely structured information than traditional programs. PIMs vary widely, but all attempt to manage information the way people use it in their jobs.

pin (1) Male lead on a connecting plug (serial port, monitor cable, keyboard connector, etc.) or the spiderlike foot on a chip. Each pin is plugged into a socket to complete the circuit.

(2) (PIN) (**P**ersonal **I**dentification **N**umber) Personal password used for identification purposes.

pin compatible All connecting signal lines are compatible.

PINS

pin feed Method for moving paper that contains a set of pins on a platen or tractor. The pins engage the paper through perforated holes in its sides. See *tractor feed*.

pinouts Description and purpose of each pin in a connector.

pipeline processing Category of techniques that provide simultaneous, or parallel, processing within the computer It refers to overlapping operations by moving data or instructions into a conceptual pipe with all stages of the pipe processing simultaneously. For example, while one instruction is being executed, the computer is decoding the next instruction. In vector processors, several steps in a floating point operation can be processed simultaneously.

PIN FEED

piracy Illegal copying of software for personal or commercial use.

pitch Number of printed characters per inch. With proportionally spaced characters, the pitch is variable and must be measured as an average. See *dot pitch*.

pixel (**PIX** [picture] **EL**ement) Smallest element on a video display screen. A screen is broken up into thousands of tiny dots, and a pixel is one or more dots that are treated as a unit. A pixel can be one dot on a monochrome screen, three dots (red, green and blue) on color screens, or clusters of these dots.

plasma display Also called *gas discharge*, a flat-screen technology that contains an inert ionized gas sandwiched between x- and y-axis panels. A pixel is selected by charging one x- and one y-wire, causing the gas in that vicinity to glow a bright orange.

platen Long, thin cylinder in a typewriter or printer that guides the paper through it and serves as a backstop for the printing mechanism to bang into.

platform Hardware architecture of a particular model or computer family. It is the standard to which software developers write their programs. The term may also include the operating system. See *environment*.

platter One of the disks in a disk pack or hard disk drive. Each platter provides a top and bottom recording surface.

plotter Graphics printer that draws images with ink pens. It requires data in vector graphics format, which makes up an image as a series of point-to-point lines.

plug compatible Hardware that is designed to perform exactly like another vendor's product. A plug compatible CPU runs the same software as the machine it's compatible with. A plug compatible peripheral works the same as the device it's replacing.

pocket computer Hand-held, calculator-sized computer that runs on batteries. It can be plugged into a personal computer for data transfer.

point and shoot To select a menu option or activate a function by moving the cursor onto a line or object and pressing the return key or mouse button.

point of sale Capturing data at the time and place of sale. Point of sale systems use personal computers or specialized terminals that are combined with cash registers, optical scanners for reading product tags, and/or magnetic stripe readers for reading credit cards.

pointer (1) On-screen symbol used to identify menu selections or the current screen location. It is moved by a mouse or other pointing device.

(2) In database management, an address embedded within the data that specifies the location of data in another record or file.

(3) In programming, a variable that is used as a reference to the current item in a table (array) or to some other object, such as the current row or column on screen.

pointing device Input device, such as a mouse or graphics tablet, used to move the cursor on screen or to draw an image.

polling Communications technique that determines when a terminal is ready to send data. The computer continually interrogates its terminals in a round robin sequence. If a terminal has data to send, it sends back an acknowledgement and the transmission begins.

popup (1) Type of menu displayed on top of the existing text or image. When the item is selected, the menu disappears and the screen is restored.

(2) Same as TSR.

port (1) Pathway into and out of the computer. The serial and parallel ports on a personal computer are external sockets for plugging in communications lines, modems and printers.

(2) To convert software to run in a different computer environment.

portable computer Personal computer that can be easily transported. Compared to desktop models, it has limited expansion slots and disk capacity.

portrait Orientation in which the data is printed across the narrow side of the form.

POS See *point of sale.*

POST (**P**ower **O**n **S**elf **T**est) Series of built-in diagnostics that are performed when the computer is first started. Proprietary codes are generated (POST codes) that indicate test results. See *diagnostic board.*

PostScript Page description language from Adobe Systems, Inc., Mountain View, CA, used in a wide variety of printers, imagesetters and display systems.

PostScript commands do not drive the printer directly. They are language statements (ASCII text) that are translated into the printer's machine language by a PostScript interpreter built into the printer. Fonts are scaled to size by the interpreter, thus eliminating the need to store a variety of font sizes on disk.

PostScript Level 2, downward compatible with original PostScript, adds data compression and enhancements, especially for color printing.

PostScript fonts come in Type 1 and Type 3 formats, and Adobe makes only Type 1. Type 1 fonts are widely used and are made by other companies as Adobe later made the format public.

power down To turn off the computer in an orderly manner by making sure all applications have been closed normally and then shutting the power.

power supply Electrical system that converts AC current from the wall outlet into the DC currents required by the computer circuitry.

power up To turn the computer on in an orderly manner.

power user Person who is very proficient with personal computers. It implies knowledge of a variety of software packages.

PowerPC RISC chip from Motorola for IBM/Apple's joint venture.

ppm (Pages Per Minute) Measures the speed of a page printer, such as a laser printer.

precision Number of digits used to express the fractional part of a number. The more digits, the more precision.

preemptive multitasking Multitasking that shares processing time with all running programs. For example, background programs can be given recurrent CPU time no matter how heavy the foreground load. Contrast with *non-preemtive multitasking*.

presentation graphics Business graphics, such as bar charts and graphs, that are used as presentation material in meetings and lectures. It implies the ability to create stylized graphics such as 3-D charts.

Presentation Manager Graphical user interface in OS/2.

preventive maintenance Routine checking of hardware that is performed by a field engineer on a regularly scheduled basis.

print image Text or graphics document that has been prepared for the printer. Format codes for the required printer have been embedded in the document at the appropriate places. Headers, footers and page numbers have been created and inserted into every page of text.

print queue Disk space that holds output designated for the printer until the printer can receive it.

print screen Ability to print the current on-screen image. See *screen dump*.

print server Computer in a network that controls one or more printers. It stores the print-image output from all users of the system and feeds it to the printers.

print spooler Software that allows printing to take place in the background while other tasks are being performed in the foreground.

printed circuit board Flat board that holds chips and other electronic components. The board is "printed" with electrically conductive pathways between components. The main printed circuit board in a system, such as the motherboard, is called a *board*, while the smaller ones that plug into the slots in the main board are called *boards* or *cards*.

printer Device that converts computer output into printed images. The most widely used personal computer printers are dot matrix printers and laser printers.

printer buffer Memory device that accepts printer output from one or more computers and transmits it to the printer. It lets the computer dispose of its printer output at full speed without waiting for each page to print. Printer buffers with automatic switching are connected to two or more computers and accept their output on a first-come, first-served basis.

PRINTED CIRCUIT BOARD
(Courtesy Rockewell International)
This board contains a 9600 bps modem.

printer cable Wire that connects a printer to a computer. On a PC, the cable has a 25-pin DB-25 male connector for the computer and a 36-pin Centronics male connector for the printer.

printer engine Unit within the printer that does the actual printing. For example, in a laser printer, it is the "copy machine" unit, which transfers and fuses the toner onto the paper. It is specified by its resolution and speed.

privacy Authorized distribution of information (who has a right to know?). Contrast with *security*, which deals with unauthorized access to data.

procedural language Programming language that requires programming discipline, such as COBOL, FORTRAN, BASIC, C, Pascal and dBASE. Programmers writing in such languages must develop a proper order of actions in order to solve the problem, based on a knowledge of data processing and programming. Contrast with *non-procedural language*. The following dBASE example lists a file from beginning to end.

```
        Procedural                    Non-procedural (interactive)
use customer
do while .not. eof                    use customer
? name, amountdue                     list name, amountdue
skip
enddo
```

procedure (1) Manual procedures are human tasks.

(2) Machine procedures are lists of routines or programs to be executed, such as described by the job control language (JCL) in a mini or mainframe, or batch files in a personal computer.

process To manipulate data in the computer. The computer is said to be processing no matter what action is taken upon the data. It may be updated or simply displayed on screen.

process bound Excessive amount of processing causing an imbalance between I/O and processing. Process-bound applications may slow down other users in a multiuser system. A personal computer is process bound when it is recalculating a spreadsheet, for example.

process control Automated control of a process, such as a manufacturing process or assembly line. It is used extensively in industrial operations, such as oil refining, chemical processing and electrical generation.

processing Manipulating data within the computer. The term is used to define a variety of computer functions and methods. See *centralized processing, distributed processing, batch processing, transaction processing* and *multiprocessing*.

processor Same as *CPU*.

PRODIGY See *online services*.

program Collection of instructions that tell the computer what to do. A program is called *software*; hence, program, software and instructions are synonymous.

program logic Sequence of instructions in a program. There are many logical solutions to a problem. If you give a specification to ten programmers, each one may create program logic that is slightly different than all the rest, but the results can be the same. The solution that runs the fastest is usually the most desired, however.

programmable Capable of following instructions. What sets the computer apart from all other electronic devices is its programmability.

programmer Person who designs the logic for and writes the lines of codes of a computer program. See *application programmer* and *systems programmer*.

programmer analyst Person who analyzes and designs information systems and designs and writes the application programs for the system. A programmer analyst is both systems analyst and applications programmer.

programming Creating a computer program. The steps are:
1. Developing the program logic to solve the particular problem.
2. Writing the program logic in a specific programming language (coding).
3. Assembling or compiling the program to turn it into machine language.
4. Testing and debugging the program.
5. Preparing the necessary documentation.
The logic is the most difficult part of programming. Writing the language statements is comparatively easy once the solution has been developed. However, regardless of how difficult the program may be, documenting it is considered the most annoying activity by most programmers.

programming languages Language used to write instructions for the computer. It lets the programmer express data processing in a symbolic manner without regard to machine-specific details. Following are the most popular programming languages.

Low-level Languages
There is an assembly language, or low-level language, for every machine type, which usually generates one machine instruction for each assembly language instruction. Assembly languages are often very different and hard to convert from one to the other.

High-level Languages

High-level languages allow the problem to expressed at a higher level than the machine level. They are called compiler languages, and they can be compiled (translated) into machine language for a variety of different computer families. Following is a list of the major high-level languages that have been used.

Ada - Comprehensive, Pascal-based language developed by the Dept. of Defense.

ALGOL - International language for expressing algorithms. Mostly used in Europe.

APL - Used for statistics and mathematical matrices. Requires special keyboard symbols.

BASIC - Developed as a timesharing language in the 1960s, it is widely used in microcomputer programming.

C - Developed in the 1980s at AT&T, it is widely used to develop commercial applications. UNIX is written in C. C++ is an object-oriented version of C that is becoming very popular.

COBOL - Developed in the 1960s, it is widely used for minicomputer and mainframe programming. It is also available for personal computers.

dBASE - The dBASE language became a de facto standard business application language with offshoots, such as Clipper and FoxBase, known as the "Xbase" languages.

FORTH - Used in process control and game applications. Provides direct control of the computer.

FORTRAN - Developed in 1954 by IBM, it was the first major scientific programming language. Some commercial applications have been developed in it however.

LISP - Developed in 1960, LISP is used to program AI applications. Its syntax is very different than other languages.

Logo - Developed in the 1960s, it includes "turtle graphics," which draws graphic elements by stating the geometry of the pen (go forward 100 units, turn right 45 degrees).

Modula-2 - Enhanced version of Pascal developed in 1979 by Nicklaus Wirth, creator of Pascal.

MUMPS - Originally Massachusetts Utility MultiProgramming System, it includes its own database and is widely used in medical applications.

Pascal - Originally an academic language in the 1970s, Borland made it a commercial success with its Turbo Pascal. Pascal uses features later copied by other languages.

Prolog - Developed in France in 1973, it is used throughout Europe and Japan for AI applications.

REXX - Running under IBM mainframes, it is used as a general purpose macro language that can send commands to application programs and operating systems.

PROM (**P**rogrammable **R**ead **O**nly **M**emory) Permanent memory chip that is programmed, or filled, by the customer rather than by the chip manufacturer. Contrast with *ROM*, which is programmed at the time of manufacture.

PROM blower Same as *PROM programmer*.

PROM programmer Device that writes instructions and data into PROM and/or EPROM chips. The bits in a new PROM are all 1s (continuous lines). The PROM programmer only creates 0s, by "blowing" the middle out of the 1s.

PROM PROGRAMMER

prompt Software message that requests action by the user; for example, "Enter employee name." Command-driven systems issue a cryptic symbol when ready to accept a command; for example, in dBASE it is simply a dot (.), in UNIX, a $, and in DOS, the venerable C:\>.

Protected Mode In Intel 286s and up, an operational state that allows the computer to address all of memory. It also prevents one program from entering into the memory boundary of another, thus enabling multiple programs to run in a guarded environment.

protocol See *communications protocol* and *OSI*.

prototyping Creating a demo of a new system. Prototyping has become essential for clarifying information requirements. Using fourth-generation languages, systems analysts and users can develop the new system together. Databases can be created and manipulated while the user monitors the progress.

PS/1 IBM home computer series introduced in 1990 that features an integrated monitor and easy-to-open case. Original models use the 286 CPU and PC bus.

PS/2 IBM personal computer series introduced in 1987 that supersedes the original PC line. It features the 3.5" microfloppy disk, VGA graphics and Micro Channel bus. The 3.5" disks and VGA are now common in all PCs and Micro Channel PCs are offered by some non-IBM vendors. Smaller PS/2 models use the original PC bus.

pseudo language Intermediate language generated from a source language, but not directly executable by a CPU. It must be interpreted or compiled into machine language for execution. It facilitates using one source language for different computers.

public domain software Software in which ownership has been relinquished to the public at large. See *shareware*.

pull-down menu Also called a pop-down menu, a menu that is displayed from the top of the screen downward when its title is selected. The menu remains displayed while the mouse button is depressed. To select a menu option, the highlight bar is moved by the mouse to the appropriate line and the mouse button is let go.

punched card First data processing storage medium, made of thin cardboard stock that holds data as patterns of punched holes.

QBE (**Q**uery **B**y **E**xample) Method for describing a query originally developed by IBM for mainframes. A replica of an empty record is displayed and the search conditions are typed in under their respective columns. The following query selects all Pennsylvania records that have a balance due of $5000 or more.

QEMM-386
Popular DOS memory manager (EMM) for 386s and up from Quarterdeck Office Systems, Santa Monica, CA. It is also part of DESQview 386.

CUSTOMER FILE

NAME	ADDRESS	CITY	STATE	ZIP	BALANCE
			PA		>=5000

QUERY BY EXAMPLE

QIC (**Q**uarter **I**nch **C**artridge Drive Standards, Inc.)
International trade association that develops standards for 1/4" (6.35mm) magnetic tape drives and cartridges used extensively for backup.

QuarkXpress Desktop publishing program for the Macintosh and Windows from Quark, Inc., Denver, CO. Originally developed for the Mac, it is noted for its precise typographic control and text and graphics manipulation.

quartz crystal Slice of quartz ground to a prescribed thickness that vibrates at a steady frequency when stimulated by electricity. The tiny crystal, about 1/20th by 1/5th of an inch, creates the computer's heartbeat.

Quattro Pro PC spreadsheet from Borland that provides advanced graphics and presentation capabilities. It has an optional interface that is keystroke, macro and file compatible with Lotus 1-2-3.

query To interrogate a database (count, sum and list selected records). Contrast with *report*, which is usually a more elaborate printout with headings and page numbers. The report may also be a selective list of items; hence, the two terms may refer to programs that produce the same results.

query by example See *QBE*.

query language Generalized language that allows a user to select records from a database. It uses a command language, menu-driven method or a query by example (QBE) format for expressing the matching condition.

Query languages are usually included in DBMSs, and stand-alone packages are available for interrogating files in non-DBMS applications.

query program Software that counts, sums and retrieves selected records from a database. It may be part of a large application and be limited to one or two kinds of retrieval, such as pulling up a customer account on screen, or it may refer to a query language that allows any condition to be searched and selected.

queue Pronounced "Q." Temporary holding place for data. See *print queue*.

quit To exit the current program. It's a good habit to quit a program before turning the computer off. Some programs don't close all files properly until quit is activated.

qwerty keyboard Standard English language typewriter keyboard. Q, w, e, r, t and y are the letters on the top left, alphabetic row. It was originally designed to slow typing to prevent the keys from jamming. See *Dvorak keyboard*.

QWERTY KEYBOARD

Computer Words You Gotta Know

radio buttons Series of on-screen buttons that allow only one selection. If a button is currently selected, it will de-select when another button is selected.

RAID (**R**edundant **A**rrays of **I**nexpensive **D**isks) Cluster of disks in which data is copied onto multiple drives. It provides faster throughput, fault tolerance (mirroring) and error correction.

RAM (**R**andom **A**ccess **M**emory) Computer's primary workspace. Also true of most memory chips (ROMs, PROMs, etc.), "random" means that the contents of each byte can be directly accessed without regard to the bytes before or after it. RAM chips require power to maintain their content. See *dynamic RAM, static RAM* and *memory*.

RAM cache See *cache*.

RAM disk Disk drive simulated in memory. To use it, files are copied from magnetic disk into the RAM disk. Processing is faster, because there's no mechanical disk action, only memory transfers. Updated data files must be copied back to disk before the power is turned off, otherwise the updates are lost.

RAM resident Refers to programs that remain in memory in order to interact with other programs or to be instantly popped up when required by the user. See *TSR*.

raster graphics In computer graphics, a technique for representing a picture image as a matrix of dots. It is the digital counterpart of the analog method used in TV. However, unlike TV, which uses one standard, there are many raster graphics standards. Contrast with *vector graphics*.

rasterize To perform the conversion of vector graphics images, vector fonts or outline fonts into bitmaps for display or printing. Unless output is printed on a plotter, which uses vectors directly, all non-bitmapped images must be rasterized into bitmaps for display or printing. See *font scaler*.

read To input into the computer from a peripheral device (disk, tape, etc.). Like reading a book or playing an audio tape, reading does not destroy what is read.

read error Failure to read the data on a storage or memory device. Magnetic and optical recording surfaces can become contaminated with dust or dirt or be physically damaged, and cells in memory chips can malfunction.

read only (1) Refers to storage media that permanently hold their content; for example, ROM and CD ROM.

(2) File which can be read, but not updated or erased. See *file attribute*.

read-only attribute File attribute that, when turned on, indicates that a file can only be read, but not updated or erased.

read/write (1) Refers to a device that can both input and output or transmit and receive.

(2) Refers to a file that can be updated and erased.

read/write head Device that reads (senses) and writes (records) data on a magnetic disk or tape.

reader Machine that captures data for the computer, such as an optical character reader, magnetic card reader and punched card reader. A microfiche or microfilm reader is a self-contained machine that reads film and displays its contents.

readme file Text file copied onto software distribution disks that contains last-minute updates or errata that have not been printed in the documentation manual.

readout (1) Small display device that typically shows only a few digits or a couple of lines of data.

(2) Any display screen or panel.

Real Mode Operational state in Intel 286s and up in which the computer functions as an 8086/8088 (XT). It is limited to one megabyte of memory. See *Protected Mode* and *Virtual 8086 Mode*.

realtime Immediate response. It refers to process control and embedded systems; for example, space flight computers must respond instantly to changing conditions. It also refers to fast transaction processing systems as well as any electronic operation fast enough to keep up with its real-world counterpart (animating complex images, transmitting live video, etc.).

realtime clock Electronic circuit that maintains the time of day. It may also provide timing signals for timesharing operations.

realtime compression Quickly compressing and decompressing data. PC products such as Stacker and SuperStor let you create a separate compressed drive on your hard disk. All data written to that drive is compressed and decompressed when read back. See *JPEG*.

realtime system Computer system that responds to input signals fast enough to keep an operation moving at its required speed.

reboot To reload the operating system and restart the computer. See *boot*.

receiver Device that accepts signals. Contrast with *transmitter*.

record (1) Group of related fields that store data about a subject (master record) or activity (transaction record). A collection of records make up a file.

Master records contain permanent data, such as account number, and variable data, such as balance due. Transaction records contain only permanent data, such as quantity and product code.

(2) In certain disk organization methods, a record is a block of data read and written at one time without any relationship to records in a file.

record layout Format of a data record, which includes the name, type and size of each field in the record.

NAME	ADDRESS	CITY	STATE	ZIP	
Conrad, James R.	809 Garibaldi Lane	Benton Falls	TN	37255-0265	

RECORD LAYOUT
RECORD LAYOUT

record locking See *file and record locking.*

reentrant code
Programming routine that can be used by multiple programs simultaneously. It is used in operating systems and other system software as well as in multithreading, where concurrent events are taking place.

refresh rate (1) Number of times per second that a device is re-energized, such as a CRT or dynamic RAM chip. See *vertical scan frequency.*

(2) In computer graphics, the time it takes to redraw or redisplay an image on screen.

register Small, high-speed computer circuit that holds values of internal operations, such as the address of the instruction being executed and the data being processed. When debugging a program, register contents may be analyzed to determine the computer's status at the time of failure.

relational database Database organization method that determines relationships between files when required. Rather than having fixed, pre-determined links, or pointers, between files (customers to orders, vendors to purchases, etc.), a relational database links files by comparing. It has the flexibility to take any two or more files and generate a new file from the records that meet the matching criteria.

remote control software Software that allows a user at one computer to interact with a computer in a different location as if the remote computer were the local machine.

removable disk Disk unit that is inserted into its respective disk drive for reading and writing and removed when not required. Floppy disks and disk cartridges are removable disk media.

render To draw a real-world object as it actually appears.

report Printed or microfilmed collection of facts and figures with page numbers and page headings. See *query.*

report file File that describes how a report is printed.

report format Layout of a report showing page and column headers, page numbers and totals.

report generator Same as *report writer.*

report writer Software that prints a report based on a description of the layout. As a stand-alone program or part of a DBMS, it retrieves selected records from a file and may sort them into a new sequence before printing.
   Developed in the early 1970s, report writers, or report generators as they were originally called, were the precursor to today's query languages and were the first programs to generate computer output without having to be programmed.

repository Database of information about applications software that includes author, data elements, inputs, processes, outputs and interrelationships. It may be the central core of a CASE system; for example, Repository Manager in IBM's AD/Cycle is designed to integrate third-party CASE products.

reserved word Verb or noun in a programming or command language that is part of the language. Its name may not be allowed for user-defined variables.

resolution Degree of sharpness of a displayed or printed character or image. On screen, resolution is expressed as a matrix of dots. VGA resolution of 640x480 means 640 dots across each of 480 lines. Sometimes the number of colors are added to the spec; for example, 640x480x16 or 640x480x256. The same resolution looks sharper on a small screen than a large one.

COLUMNS OF
RESOLUTION

↓

640 x 480

↑

ROWS OF
RESOLUTION

For printers, resolution is expressed as the number of dots per linear inch. A 300 dpi resolution means 90,000 dots per square inch (300x300).

response time Time it takes for the computer to comply with a user's request, such as looking up a customer record.

return key Also called the enter key, the large key on the right side of the keyboard. It is used to end a paragraph of text or line of data.

RF (**R**adio **F**requency) Range of electromagnetic frequencies that all broadcast transmission, from AM radio to satellites, falls into. Often refers to antenna input or a video signal transmitted via a TV channel.

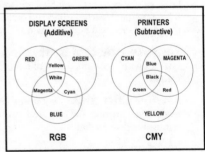

RGB (**R**ed **G**reen **B**lue) Video color generation method that displays colors as varying intensities of red, green and blue dots. When all three are turned on high, white is produced. As intensities are equally lowered, shades of gray are derived. The base color of the screen appears when all dots are off. See CMYK.

RGB AND CMY COLOR MIXING

RGB monitor (1) Video display screen that requires separate red, green and blue signals from the computer. It generates a better image than composite signals (TV) which merge the three colors together. It comes in both analog and digital varieties.

(2) Sometimes refers to a CGA monitor that accepts digital RGB signals.

ribbon cable Thin, flat, multiconductor cable that is widely used in electronic systems; for example, to interconnect peripheral devices to the computer internally.

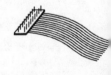

RIBBON CABLE

RIP (**R**aster **I**mage **P**rocessor) In computer graphics, the component (hardware, software or both) that prepares data for a raster output device (screen or printer). RIPs are designed for a specific type of input, such as vectors, PostScript as well as different raster data.

RISC (**R**educed **I**nstruction **S**et **C**omputer) Computer architecture that reduces the complexity of the chip by using simpler instructions. RISC compilers have to generate software routines to perform complex instructions that were previously done in hardware by traditional computers.

RJE (**R**emote **J**ob **E**ntry) Transmitting batches of transactions from a remote terminal or computer. The receiving computer processes the data and may transmit the results back to the RJE site for printing.

RLL (**R**un **L**ength **L**imited) Magnetic disk encoding method that packs 50% more bits into the same space than the earlier MFM method. It is used with RLL, IDE, ESDI, SCSI, SMD and IPI interfaces.

RLL interface See *ST506 RLL*.

robot Stand-alone hybrid computer system that performs physical and computational activities. It is a multiple-motion device with one or more arms and joints that is capable of performing many different tasks like a human. It can be designed similar to human form, although most industrial robots don't resemble people at all.

ROM (**R**ead **O**nly **M**emory) Memory chip that permanently stores instructions and data. Its contents are created at the time of manufacture and cannot be altered. Used extensively to store control routines in personal computers (ROM BIOS) and in peripheral controllers, it is also used in plug-in cartridges for printers, video games and other systems. See *PROM, EPROM* and *EEPROM*.

ROM BIOS (ROM **B**asic **I**nput **O**utput **S**ystem) Instructions contained in a ROM chip that activate peripheral devices in a PC. It includes routines for the keyboard, screen, disk, parallel and serial port and for internal services such as time and date. It accepts requests from the device drivers in the operating system as well as from application programs.

ROM card Credit-card-sized module that contains permanent software or data. See *memory card*.

root directory In hierarchical file systems, the starting point in the hierarchy. When the computer is first started, the root directory is the current directory. Access to directories in the hierarchy requires naming the directories that are in its path. See *path*.

router In communications, a device that examines the destination address of a message and selects the most effective route. It is used in complex networks where there are many pathways between users. See *bridge* and *gateway*.

routine Set of instructions that perform a task. Same as *module* and *procedure*.

RPC (**R**emote **P**rocedure **C**all) Type of interface that allows one program to call another in a remote location. Using a standard RPC allows an application to be used in a variety of networks without change.

RPG (**R**eport **P**rogram **G**enerator) One of the first program generators designed for business reports, introduced in 1964 by IBM. In 1970, RPG II added enhancements that made it a mainstay programming language for business applications on IBM's System/3x midrange computers. RPG III, which added more programming structures, is widely used on the AS/400. RPG statements are written in columnar format.

RS-232-C EIA standard for a serial interface between computers and peripheral devices (modem, mouse, etc.). It uses a 25-pin DB-25 or 9-pin DB-9 connector. Its normal cable limitation of 50 feet can be extended to several hundred feet with high-quality cable.

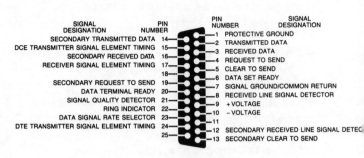

SIGNAL DESIGNATION	PIN NUMBER
SECONDARY TRANSMITTED DATA	14
DCE TRANSMITTER SIGNAL ELEMENT TIMING	15
SECONDARY RECEIVED DATA	16
RECEIVER SIGNAL ELEMENT TIMING	17
	18
SECONDARY REQUEST TO SEND	19
DATA TERMINAL READY	20
SIGNAL QUALITY DETECTOR	21
RING INDICATOR	22
DATA SIGNAL RATE SELECTOR	23
DTE TRANSMITTER SIGNAL ELEMENT TIMING	24
	25

PIN NUMBER	SIGNAL DESIGNATION
1	PROTECTIVE GROUND
2	TRANSMITTED DATA
3	RECEIVED DATA
4	REQUEST TO SEND
5	CLEAR TO SEND
6	DATA SET READY
7	SIGNAL GROUND/COMMON RETURN
8	RECEIVED LINE SIGNAL DETECTOR
9	+VOLTAGE
10	–VOLTAGE
11	
12	SECONDARY RECEIVED LINE SIGNAL DETEC
13	SECONDARY CLEAR TO SEND

RS-232 PINOUTS
(Courtesy Black Box Corporation)

RSI (**R**epetitive **S**train **I**njury) Ailments of the hands, neck, back and eyes due to computer use. The remedy for RSI is frequent breaks which should include stretching or yoga postures. See *carpal tunnel syndrome.*

RTFM (**R**ead **T**he **F**laming **M**anual) Last resort when having a hardware or software problem!

run (1) To execute a program.

(2) Single or multiple programs scheduled for execution.

runtime version Software that is combined with an application so that it can run as a stand-alone program or run with enhanced features. Many applications are developed under DBMSs that require the DBMS to be running in the computer in order to run the application. Runtime versions of those applications allow them to run in computers that don't have the DBMS.

A runtime version of Digital Research's GEM graphical interface accompanies the DOS version of the Ventura Publisher desktop publishing program, giving that application its graphical interface.

In the early days of Windows, some applications were packaged with runtime versions of Windows, allowing them to use the features of the Windows interface in computers that didn't have Windows installed. In such cases, normal Windows applications could not be executed.

S/3x See *System/3x*.

S/360 See *System/360*.

S/370 See *System/370*.

S3 chip Refers to one of the graphics accelerator chips from S3, Inc., San Jose, CA, used in a variety of graphics accelerator boards.

SAA (**S**ystem **A**pplication **A**rchitecture) Introduced in 1987, a set of IBM standards (user interfaces, programming interfaces and communications protocols) that provide consistency across all IBM platforms. Categories are Common User Access (CUA), Common Programming Interface (CPI) and Common Communications Support (CCS).

sampling rate In digitizing operations, the frequency with which samples are taken and converted. The higher the sample rate, the closer real-world objects are represented in digital form.

save To write the contents of memory to disk or tape. Some applications save data automatically, others do not. Memory-based word processors, and most all spreadsheets require that the user saves the data before exiting the program.

scalable font Font that is created in the required point size when needed to display or print a document. The dot patterns (bitmaps) are generated from a set of outline fonts, or base fonts, which contain a mathematical representation of the typeface. Scalable fonts eliminate storing dozens of different font sizes on disk. Contrast with *bitmapped font*. See *font scaler*.

scale (1) In computer graphics and printing, to resize an object, making it smaller or larger.

(2) To change the representation of a quantity in order to bring it into prescribed limits of another range. For example, values such as 1249, 876, 523, -101 and -234 might need to be scaled into a range from -5 to +5.

(3) To designate the position of the decimal point in a fixed or floating point number.

scan (1) In optical technologies, to view a printed form a line at a time in order to convert images into bitmapped representations, or to convert characters into ASCII text or some other data code.

(2) In video, to move across a picture frame a line at a time, either to detect the image in an analog or digital camera, or to refresh a CRT display.

(3) To sequentially search a file.

scan rate Number of times per second a scanning device samples its field of vision. See *horizontal scan frequency*.

scanner Device that reads text, images and bar codes. Text and bar code scanners recognize printed fonts and bar codes and convert them into a digital code (ASCII or EBCDIC). Graphics scanners convert a printed image into a video image (raster graphics) without recognizing the actual content of the text or pictures.

scientific applications Applications that simulate real-world activities using mathematics. Real-world objects are turned into mathematical models and their actions are simulated by executing the formulas.

scientific language Programming language designed for mathematical formulas and matrices, such as ALGOL, FORTRAN and APL. Although all programming languages allow for this kind of processing, statements in a scientific language make it easier to express these actions.

scientific notation Display of numbers in floating point form. The number (mantissa) is always equal to or greater than one and less than 10, and the base is 10. For example, 2.345E6 is equivalent to 2,345,000. The number following E (exponent) represents the power to which the base should be raised (number of zeros following the decimal point).

SCO Open Desktop Multiuser, virtual memory graphical operating system for 386s and up from The Santa Cruz Operation that runs UNIX, XENIX, DOS and X Window applications.

screen dump Printing the current on-screen image. In PCs, pressing Shift-PrtSc prints the screen. If the screen contains graphics, the DOS Graphics utility must be loaded. Third party screen capture programs also dump graphic screens to the printer or to disk.
    In the Macintosh, pressing Command-shift-3 creates a MacPaint file of the current screen.

screen saver Utility that prevents a CRT from being etched by an unchanging image. After a specified duration without keyboard or mouse input, it blanks the screen or displays moving objects. Pressing a key or moving the mouse restores the screen.
    It would actually take many hours to burn in an image on today's color monitors. However, the entertainment provided by these utilities (swimming fish, flying toasters, etc.) has made them very popular.

script (1) Typeface that looks like handwriting or calligraphy.

(2) Program or macro.

scroll To continuously move forward, backward or sideways through the images on screen or within a window. Scrolling implies continuous and smooth movement, a line, character or pixel at a time, as if the data were on a paper scroll being rolled behind the screen.

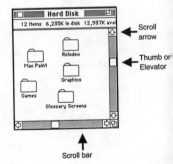

scroll arrow On-screen arrow that is clicked in order to scroll the screen in the corresponding direction. The screen moves one line, or increment, with each mouse click.

scroll bar Horizontal or vertical bar that contains a box that looks like an elevator in a shaft. The bar is clicked to scroll the screen in the corresponding direction, or the box (elevator, thumb) is clicked and then dragged to the desired direction.

scrollable See *scroll*.

scrollable field Short line on screen that can be scrolled to allow editing or display of larger amounts of data in a small display space.

SCSI (**S**mall **C**omputer **S**ystem **I**nterface) Pronounced "scuzzy." An interface for up to seven peripherals (disk, tape, CD ROM, etc.). It is an 8-bit bus interface for up to eight devices, but the host adapter, which connects to the computer's bus, also counts as a device. The SCSI bus allows any two devices to communicate at one time (host to peripheral, peripheral to peripheral). Macintoshes come with built-in SCSI host adapters.

scuzzy See *SCSI*.

seamless integration Addition of a new application, routine or device that works smoothly with the existing system. It implies that the new feature can be activated and used without problems. Contrast with *transparent*, which implies that there is no discernible change after installation.

second-generation computer Computer made of discrete electronic components. In the early 1960s, the IBM 1401 and Honeywell 400 were examples.

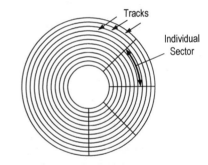

sector Smallest unit of storage read or written on a disk. Sectors are fixed in length, and the same number of sectors usually reside in one track. However, the hardware may vary the disk speed to fit more sectors into tracks located on the outer edges of the disk platter. The sector is the physical unit called for by an instruction, for example, READ TRACK 17 SECTOR 23.

sector interleave Sector numbering on a hard disk. A one to one interleave (1:1) is sequential: 0,1,2,3, etc. 2:1 staggers sectors as follows: 0,4,1,5,2,6,3,7. The best interleave uses fewest disk rotations to access contiguous sectors.

SECTORS ON A DISK

security Protection of data against unauthorized access. Programs and data can be secured by issuing identification numbers and passwords to authorized users of a computer. However, systems programmers, or other technically competent individuals, will ultimately have access to these codes.

seek time Time it takes to move the read/write head to a particular track on a disk after the instruction has been executed.

self-extracting file One or more compressed files that have been converted into an executable program which decompresses its contents when run.

semiconductor Solid state substance that switches from non-conductive to conductive when charged with electricity or light. The common semiconductor device is the silicon transistor, simply an on/off switch.

sequential access method Organizing data in an ascending or descending sequence. Searching sequential data requires reading and comparing each record, starting from the top or bottom of file.

serial mouse See *bus mouse*.

serial port I/O connector used to attach a modem, mouse, scanner or other serial interface device to the computer. The typical serial port uses a DB-25 or DB-9 connector, which on the back of a PC is a 25-pin male or 9-pin male connector. Contrast with *parallel port*.

serial printer Type of printer that prints one character at a time, in contrast to a line or page at a time. In this context, serial has no relationship to a serial or parallel interface that is used to attach the printer to the computer.

serial transmission Transmitting data over one line, one bit at a time. Contrast with *parallel transmission*.

server Computer in a network shared by multiple users. See *file server* and *print server*.

service Functionality derived from a particular software program. For example, network services may refer to programs that transmit data or provide conversion of data in a network. Database services provides for the storage and retrieval of data in a database.

service bureau Organization that provides data processing and timesharing services. It may offer a variety of software packages, batch processing services (data entry, COM, etc.) as well as custom programming.

Customers pay for storage of data on the system and processing time used. Connection is made to a service bureau through dial-up terminals, private lines, or other networks, such as Telenet or Tymnet.

session (1) In communications, the active connection between a user and a computer or between two computers.

(2) Using an application program (period between starting up and quitting).

setup program Software that configures a system for a particular environment. It is used to install a new application and modify it when the hardware changes. When used with expansion boards, it may change the hardware by altering on-board memory chips (flash memory, EEPROMs, etc.). See *install program*.

shadow batch Data collection system that simulates a transaction processing environment. Instead of updating master files (customers, inventory, etc.) when orders or shipments are initiated, the transactions are stored in the computer. When a user makes a query, the master record from the previous update cycle is retrieved; but before it's displayed, it's updated in memory with any transactions that may affect it. The up-to-date master record is then displayed for the user. At the end of the day or period, the transactions are then actually batch processed against the master file.

shadow mask Screen full of holes that adheres to the back of a color CRT's viewing glass. The electron beam is aimed through the holes onto the phosphor dots.

shadow RAM In a PC, a copy of the operating system's BIOS routines in RAM to improve performance. RAM chips are faster than ROM chips.

shareware Software distributed on a trial basis through BBS's, online services, mail-order vendors and user groups. Shareware is software on the honor system. If you use it regularly, you're required to register and pay for it, for which you will receive technical support and perhaps additional documentation or the next upgrade. Paid licenses are required for commercial distribution.

shell Outer layer of a program that provides the user interface, or way of commanding the computer. Shells are typically add-on programs created for command-driven operating systems, such as UNIX and DOS. It provides a menu-driven or graphical icon-oriented interface to the system in order to make it easier to use. DOS 4.0 and 5.0 come with their own shell (DOSshell).

shell out To temporarily exit an application, go back to the operating system, perform a function and then return to the application.

shrink-wrapped software Refers to store-bought software, implying a standard platform that is widely supported.

SI See *systems integration*.

Sidekick PC desktop utility program from Borland. Introduced in 1984, it was the first popup (TSR) program for the PC. It includes a calculator, WordStar-compatible notepad, appointment calendar, phone dialer and ASCII table.

SIG (**S**pecial **I**nterest **G**roup) Group of people that meets and shares information about a particular topic of interest. It is usally a part of a larger group or association.

signature Unique number built into hardware or software for identification. See *XyWrite III Plus*.

silicon (Si) Base material used in chips. Next to oxygen, it is the most abundant element in nature and is found in a natural state in rocks and sand. Its atomic structure makes it an ideal semiconductor material. In chip making, it is mined from rocks and put through a chemical process at high temperatures to purify it. To alter its electrical properties, it is mixed (doped) with other chemicals in a molten state.

SAN FRANCISCO

San Francisco Bay

Menlo Park • ●
Palo Alto ● Mountain View
Pacific Ocean Los Altos • • Sunnyvale
Santa Clara •
Cupertino • ●
San Jose

SILICON VALLEY

Named Silicon Valley because of the concentration of computer companies in this area south of San Francisco.

SIMM (**S**ingle **I**n-line **M**emory **M**odule) Narrow printed circuit board about three inches long that holds eight or nine memory chips. It plugs into a SIMM socket on the circuit board.
  A 1x9 designation means a 1megabyte SIMM made of 9 chips (1x3 is 1 meg, 3 chips).

simplex One way transmission. Contrast with *half-duplex* and *full-duplex*.

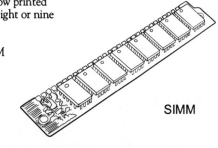

SIMM

simulation (1) Mathematical representation of the interaction of real-world objects. (2) Execution of a machine language program designed to run in a foreign computer.

SIP (**S**ingle **In**-line **P**ackage) Type of chip module that is similar to a SIMM, but uses pins rather than edge connectors. SIPs are sometimes called SIPPs (Single In-Line Pin Package).

site license License to use software within a facility. It provides authorization to make copies and distribute them within a specific jurisdiction.

smart cable Connecting cable between two devices that has a built-in microprocessor. It analyzes incoming signals and converts them from one protocol to another.

smart card Credit card with built-in microprocessor and memory used for identification or financial transactions. When inserted into a reader, it transfers data to and from a central computer. It is more secure than a magnetic stripe card and can be programmed to self-destruct if the wrong password is entered too many times. As a financial transaction card, it can store transactions and maintain a bank balance.

smart terminal Video terminal with built-in display characteristics (blinking, reverse video, underlines, etc.). It may also contain a communications protocol. Sometimes refers to intelligent terminal. See *intelligent terminal* and *dumb terminal*.

SMDS (**S**witched **M**ultimegabit **D**ata **S**ervices) High-speed data services in the 45 Mbits/sec range proposed by local telephone companies that will allow companies to build private MANs.

smoke test Test of new or repaired equipment by turning it on. If there's smoke, it doesn't work!

SNA (**S**ystems **N**etwork **A**rchitecture) IBM mainframe network standards introduced in 1974. Originally a centralized architecture with a host computer controlling many terminals, enhancements, such as APPN and APPC (LU 6.2), have adapted SNA to today's peer-to-peer communications and distributed computing environment. SNA includes software called *VTAM* (virtual telecommunications access method), *NCP* (network control program) and *SDLC* (synchronous data link protocol).

snapshot Storing the contents of memory including all hardware registers and status indicators. It is periodically taken in order to restore the system in the event of failure.

sneaker net Human alternative to a LAN. It is made up of people carrying floppy disks from one machine to another.

sniffer Software and/or hardware that detects bottlenecks and problems in a network.

SNMP (**S**imple **N**etwork **M**anagement **P**rotocol) Network management standard that originated in the UNIX community and has spread to VMS, DOS and other environments. Data is passed between SNMP agents (processes that monitor activity in hubs, routers, bridges, etc.) and the workstation used to oversee the network. MIBs (management information bases) are databases that define what information is obtainable from the network device and what can be controlled (turned off, on, etc.).

snow Flickering snow-like spots on a video screen caused by display electronics that are too slow to respond to changing data.

soft font Set of characters for a particular typeface that is stored on the computer's hard disk, or in some cases the printer's hard disk, and downloaded to the printer before printing. Contrast with *internal font* and *font cartridge*.

soft return Code inserted by the software into a text document to mark the end of the line. When the document is printed, the soft return is converted into the end-of-line code required by the printer. Soft returns are determined by the right margin and change when the margins are changed.

software Instructions for the computer. A series of instructions that performs a particular task is called a program or software program. The two major categories are *system software* and *application software*.

software house Organization that develops customized software for a customer. Contrast with *software publisher*, which develops and markets software packages.

software package Application program for sale to the general public.

software publisher Organization that develops and markets software. It does market research, production and distribution of software. It may develop its own software, contract for it or obtain existing software.

Solaris Operating environment from Sun that runs on its SPARCstations and 386s and up. It includes Sun's UNIX-based operating system, network protocols, version of X Window and the Open Look graphical interface. The x86 version runs DOS and Windows applications.

solid state Electronic component or circuit made of solid materials, such as transistors, chips and bubble memory. There is no mechanical action in a solid state device, although an unbelievable amount of electromagnetic action takes place.

solid state disk Disk drive made of memory chips used for high-speed data access or in adverse environments. They are used in battery-powered, hand-held devices as well as in units with hundreds of megabytes of storage and built-in UPS systems.

sort To reorder data into a new sequence. Sorting capabilities are provided within the operating system and many application programs, such as word processors and DBMSs.

sort key Field or fields in a record that dictate the sequence of the file. For example, the sort keys STATE and NAME arrange the file alphabetically by name within state. STATE is the major sort key, and NAME is the minor key.

sound card Personal computer expansion board that generates sound and provides outputs for external amplification and speakers. Unshielded speakers located too close to CRT screens will cause visible interference. Shielded speakers are commonly available for computer use. See MPC.

source code Collection of programming statements as written by the programmer. It must be converted into machine language by compilers, assemblers and interpreters before it can be executed (run) by the computer.

source computer Computer in which a program is being assembled or compiled. Contrast with *object computer*.

source data Original data that is handwritten or printed on a source document or typed into the computer system from a keyboard or terminal.

source disk Disk from which data is obtained. Contrast with *target disk*.

source document Paper form onto which data is written. Order forms and employment applications are examples.

source drive Disk or tape drive from which data is obtained. Contrast with *target drive*.

source language Language used in a source program.

source program Program in its original form, as written by the programmer.

space/time

Bits, bytes and cycles		Fractions of a second	
K (kilo) thousand	1,024	ms (millisecond) thousandth	1/1,000
M (mega) million	1,048,576	µs (microsecond) millionth	1/1,000,000
G (giga) billion	1,073,741,824	ns (nanosecond) billionth	1/1,000,000,000
T (tera) trillion	1,099,511,627,776	ps (picosecond) trillionth	1/1,000,000,000,000
P (peta) quadrillion	1,125,899,906,842,624	fs (femtosecond) quadrillionth	1/1,000,000,000,000,000

How Components Are Measured

Storage/channel capacity		Transmission speed	
CPU word size	bits	CPU clock speed	MHz (megahertz)
Bus size	bits	Bus speed	MHz (megahertz)
Disk, tape	bytes	Network line/channel	bps (bits per second)
MEMORY		Disk transfer rate	bps or bytes per second
Overall capacity	bytes	Disk access time	ms
SIMM or SIP module	bytes	Memory access time	ns
Individual chip	bits	Machine cycle	µs, ns
		Instruction execution	µs, ns
		Transistor switching	ns, ps, fs

spaghetti code Program code written without a coherent structure. It implies that the logic moves from routine to routine without coming back to a base point, making it very hard to follow. Contrast with *structured programming*.

SPARC (**S**calable **P**erformance **ARC**hitecture) 32-bit RISC CPU developed by Sun and licensed by SPARC International, Menlo Park, CA. It is used in Sun's SPARCstation workstations.

spawn To launch another program from the current program.

special character Non-alpha or non-numeric character, such as @, #, $, %, &, * and +.

speech synthesis Generating machine voice by arranging phonemes (k, ch, sh, etc.) into words. It is used to turn text input into spoken words for the blind. Speech synthesis performs realtime conversion without a pre-defined vocabulary, but does not create human-sounding speech. Although individual spoken words can be digitized into the computer, digitized voice takes a lot of storage, and resulting phrases still lack inflection.

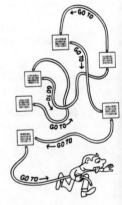

SPAGHETTI CODE

Speed Doubler See 486.

spelling checker Separate program or word processing function that tests for correctly spelled words. It can test the spelling of a marked block, an entire document or group of documents. Advanced systems check for spelling as the user types and can correct common typos and misspellings on the fly.

Spelling checkers simply compare words to a dictionary of words, and the wrong use of a correctly-spelled word cannot be detected. See *grammar checker*.

spike Also called a transient, a burst of extra voltage in a power line that lasts only a fraction of a second. See *surge*.

spooling (**S**imultaneous **P**eripheral **O**perations **O**n**L**ine) Overlapping of low-speed operations with normal processing. It originated with mainframes in order to optimize slow operations such as reading cards and printing. Card input was read onto disk and printer output was stored on disk. In that way, the actual business data processing was done at high speed, since all I/O was on disk.

Today, spooling is used to buffer data for the printer as well as remote batch terminals. See *print spooler*.

spreadsheet Software that simulates a paper spreadsheet, or worksheet, in which columns of numbers are summed for budgets and plans. It appears on screen as a matrix of rows and columns, the intersections of which are identified as cells. The spreadsheet's magic is in its ability to quickly recalculate the rows and columns whenever a change is made to the numeric data in one of the cells.

SQL (**S**tructured **Q**uery **L**anguage) Pronounced "SQL" or "see qwill," a language used to interrogate and process data in a relational database. Originally developed by IBM for its mainframes, there have been many implementations created for mini and micro database applications. SQL commands can be used to interactively work with a database or can be embedded within a programming language to interface to a database.

SQL engine Program that accepts SQL commands and accesses the database to obtain the requested data. Users' requests in a query language or database language must be translated into an SQL request before the SQL engine can process it.

S-RAM See *static RAM*.

ST506 Hard disk interface commonly used in drives 40MB and less. It transfers data at 625 KBytes/sec and uses the MFM encoding method.

ST506 RLL (ST506 **R**un-**L**ength **L**imited) Hard disk interface (also called RLL interface) that increases capacity and speed by 50% over ST506 MFM drives and transfers data at 937 KBytes/sec.

stack (1) Set of hardware registers or a reserved amount of memory used for arithmetic calculations or for keeping track of internal operations. Stacks keep track of the sequence of routines that are called in a program. For example, one routine calls another, which calls another and so on. As each routine is completed, the computer must return control to the calling routine all the way back to the first routine that started the sequence.

(2) HyperCard file.

standard Set of rules and regulations that are agreed to either by an official standards organization (de jure standard) or by general acceptance in the marketplace (de facto standard).

standards bodies

ANSI (**A**merican **N**ational **S**tandard **I**nstitute) Coordinates development of U.S. voluntary national standards, including programming languages, EDI, telecommunications and properties of disk and tape media. It is the U.S. member body of ISO. New York.

CCITT (**C**onsultative **C**ommittee for **I**nternational **T**elephony and **T**elegraphy) Communications standards. Geneva.

EIA (**E**lectronic **I**ndustries **A**ssociation) Electrical and electronic interface standards. Washington.

IEC (**I**nternational **E**lectrotechnical **C**ommission) Electrical and electronics standards. Contact via ANSI.

IEEE (**I**nstitute of **E**lectrical and **E**lectronic **E**ngineers) Standards in electronics and allied fields. New York.

ISO (**I**nternational **S**tandards **O**rganization) Many technical standards including the OSI (Open Systems Interconnet) for worldwide communications. Geneva.

JEDEC (**J**oint **E**lectronic **D**evice **E**ngineering **C**ouncil) Integrated circuit standards.

JEIDA (**J**apanese **E**lectronic **I**ndustry **D**evelopment **A**ssociation) Joined with PCMCIA to standardize on a 68-pin memory card.

NIST (**N**ational **I**nstitute of **S**tandards & **T**echnology) Standards agency of U.S. government, formerly National Bureau of Standards.

PCMCIA (**PC** **M**emory **C**ard **I**ndustry **A**ssociation) Memory card standards.

VESA (**V**ideo **E**lectronics **S**tandards **A**ssociation) Video display standards. San Jose, CA.

star network Communications network in which all terminals are connected to a central computer or central hub. PBXs are prime examples as well as IBM's Token Ring and AT&T's Starlan LANs.

start bit In asynchronous communications, the bit transmitted before each character.

start/stop transmission Same as *asynchronous transmission*.

startup routine Routine that is executed when the computer is booted or when an application is loaded. It is used to customize the environment for its associated software.

static RAM Memory chip that requires power to hold its content. Static RAM chips have access times in the 10 to 30-nanosecond range. Dynamic RAMs are usually above 30, and Bipolar and ECL memories are under 10. Static RAMs take up more space than dynamic RAMs and they use more power.

storage device Hardware unit that holds data. In this book, it refers only to external peripheral equipment, such as disk and tape, in contrast with memory (RAM).

storage media Refers to disks, tapes and bubble memory cartridges.

store and forward In communications, the temporary storage of a message for transmission to its destination at a later time. Store and forward techniques allow for routing over networks that are not accessible at all times; for example, messages headed for different time zones can be stored and forwarded when daytime arrives at the destination location. Messages can be stored and forwarded at night in order to obtain off-peak rates.

stored program concept Fundamental computer architecture in which it acts upon (executes) internally-stored instructions. See *von Neumann architecture*.

string (1) In programming, a contiguous set of alphanumeric characters that does not contain numbers used for calculations. Names, addresses, words and sentences are strings.

(2) Any connected set of structures, such as a string of bits, fields or records.

string handling Abilty to manipulate alphanumeric data (names, addresses, text, etc.). Typical functions include the ability to handle arrays of strings, to left and right align and center strings and to search for an occurrence of text within a string.

stroke font Same as *vector font*.

structured programming Variety of techniques that impose a logical structure on the writing of a program. Contrast with *spaghetti code*.

style sheet In word processing and desktop publishing, a file that contains layout settings for a particular category of document. Style sheets include such settings as margins, tabs, headers and footers, columns and fonts.

stylus Pen-shaped instrument that is used to "draw" images or point to menus. See *light pen* and *digitizer tablet*.

sub-notebook Lightweight notebook computer. As computers get lighter, the sub-notebook (if term persists) should weigh two to three pounds, the notebook four to five.

subdirectory Disk directory that is subordinate to (below) another directory. In order to gain access to a subdirectory, the path must include all directories above it.

submarining Temporary visual loss of the moving cursor on a slow display screen such as found on a laptop computer. See *active matrix LCD*.

submenu Additional list of options within a menu selection. There can many levels of submenus.

subroutine Group of instructions that perform a specific task. A large subroutine is usually called a module or procedure; a small one, a function or macro, but all terms are used interchangeably.

subschema Pronounced "sub-skeema." In database management, an individual user's partial view of the database. The schema is the entire database.

subscript (1) In word processing and mathematical notation, a digit or symbol that appears below the line. Contrast with *superscript*.

(2) Programming syntax that references an item of data in a table.

Sun See *vendors*.

supercomputer Fastest computer available. It is typically used for simulations in petroleum exploration and production, structural analysis, computational fluid dynamics, physics and chemistry, electronic design, nuclear energy research and meteorology. It is also used for realtime animated graphics.

superconductor Material that has little resistance to the flow of electricity. Traditional superconductors operate at -459 Fahrenheit (absolute zero).

superscript Any letter, digit or symbol that appears above the line. Contrast with *subscript*.

supertwist LCD display that improves on the earlier twisted numatic technology by twisting the crystals up to 180 degrees or more. It provides a wider viewing angle and improved contrast. It is recognized by its yellow and greenish blue color.

supervisor Same as *operating system*.

surface mount Circuit board packaging technique in which the leads (pins) on the chips and components are soldered on top of the board, not through it. Boards can be smaller and built faster.

surge Oversupply of voltage from the power company that can last up to several seconds. See *spike*.

surge protector Device that protects a computer from excessive voltage (spikes and surges) in the power line. See *UPS*.

surge suppressor Same as *surge protector*.

suspend and resume To stop an operation and restart where you left off. In portable computers, the hard disk is turned off, and the CPU is made to idle at its slowest speed. All open applications are retained in memory.

SVGA (super VGA) See *VGA*.

SVR4 See *System V Release 4.0*.

swap file Disk file used to temporarily save a program or part of a program running in memory.

switch (1) Mechanical or electronic device or program state that is either on or off.

(2) Modifier of a command. For example, the `/p` switch in the DOS command `dir /p` causes the directory listing to be P-aused after each screenful.

symmetric multiprocessing Multiprocessing design in which any CPU can be assigned any application task. One CPU acts as a control processor, or scheduler, which boots the system, distributes work to the next available CPU and manages I/O requests. Contrast with *asymmetric multiprocessing*.

synchronous transmission Transmission of data in which both stations are synchronized. Codes are sent from the transmitting station to the receiving station to establish the synchronization, and data is then transmitted in continuous streams. Contrast with *asynchronous transmission*.

syntax Rules governing the structure of a language statement. It specifies how words and symbols are put together to form a phrase.

syntax error Error that occurs when a program cannot understand the command that has been entered. See *parse*.

sysop (**sys**tem **op**erator) Pronounced "siss-op." Person who runs an online communications system or bulletin board. The sysop may also act as mediator for system conferences.

system (1) Group of related components that interact to perform a task.

(2) A *computer system* is made up of the CPU, operating system and peripheral devices.

(3) An *information system* is made up of the database, all the data entry, update, query and report programs and manual and machine procedures.

(4) "The system" often refers to the operating system.

System 7 Major upgrade of the Macintosh operating system (1991). It includes virtual memory, increased memory addressing, hot links, multitasking, TrueType fonts and other enhancements.

System/3x IBM System/34, System/36 and System/38 midrange computers.

System/34 Early IBM minicomputer that handled about a dozen terminals. Superseded by System/34 and System/38.

System/36 Early IBM minicomputer that handled a couple of dozen terminals. Superseded by the AS/400.

System/38 Early multiuser minicomputer from IBM that integrated a relational DBMS with the operating system.

System/360 IBM's first family of computer systems introduced in 1964. It was the first time any company announced a complete line of computers at once. The basic 360 architecture still exists in current-day IBM mainframes.

System/370 Mainframe product line introduced in 1970 by IBM (superseding System/360), which added virtual memory and other enhancements.

System/390 Mainframe product line introduced in 1990 by IBM (superseding System/370).

system development cycle Sequence of events in the development of an information system (application), which requires mutual effort on the part of user and technical staff.

   1. SYSTEMS ANALYSIS & DESIGN
     feasibility study

1. SYSTEMS ANALYSIS & DESIGN
   feasibility study
   general design
   prototyping
   detail design
   functional specifications

2. USER SIGN OFF

3. PROGRAMMING
   design
   coding
   testing

4. IMPLEMENTATION
   training
   conversion
   installation

5. USER ACCEPTANCE

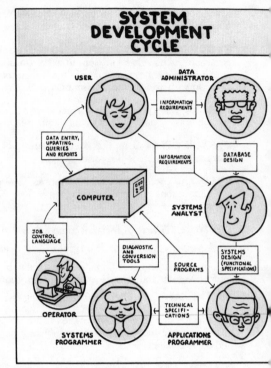

system development methodology Formal documentation for the phases of the system development cycle. It defines the precise objectives for each phase and the results required from a phase before the next one can begin. It may include specialized forms for preparing the documentation describing each phase.

system failure Hardware or software malfunction. May refer to a problem with the operating system.

SYSTEM.INI See *WIN.INI*.

system life cycle Useful life of an information system. Its length depends on the nature and volatility of the business, as well as the software development tools used to generate the databases and applications. Eventually, an information system that is patched over and over no longer is structurally sound enough to be expanded.

system software Programs used to control the computer and run application programs. It includes operating systems, TP monitors, network control programs, network operating systems and database managers. Contrast with *application program*.

system test Running a complete system for testing purposes.

System V Release 4.0 Unified version of UNIX released in 1989. See *UNIX*.

systems General term for the department, people or work involved in systems analysis & design activities.

systems analysis & design Examination of a problem and the creation of its solution. Systems analysis is effective when all sides of the problem are reviewed.

plans for the care and feeding of a new system are as important as the problems they solve. See *system development cycle*.

systems analyst Person responsible for the development of an information system. They design and modify systems by turning user requirements into a set of functional specifications, which are the blueprint of the system. They design the database or help design it if data administrators are available. They develop the manual and machine procedures and the detailed processing specs for each data entry, update, query and report program in the system.

systems engineer Often a vendor title for persons involved in consulting and pre-sales activities related to computers. See *systems analyst, systems programmer, programmer analyst* and *application programmer*.

systems house Organization that develops customized software and/or turnkey systems for customers. Contrast with *software house*, which develops software packages for sale to the general public. Both terms are used synonymously.

systems integration Making diverse components work together.

systems integrator Individual or organization that builds systems from a variety of diverse components. With increasing complexity of technology, more customers want complete solutions to information problems, requiring hardware, software and networking expertise in a multivendor environment. See *OEM* and *VAR*.

systems programmer (1) In the IS department of a large organization, a technical expert on some or all of the computer's system software (operating systems, networks, DBMSs, etc.). They are responsible for the efficient performance of the computer systems.

In mainframe environments, there is one systems programmer for about 10 or more application programmers. In smaller environments, users rely on vendors or consultants for systems programming assistance.

(2) In a computer hardware or software organization, a person who designs and writes system software.

T See *tera*.

table (1) In programming, a collection of adjacent fields. Also called an *array*, a table contains data that is either constant within the program or is called in when the program is run. See *decision table*.

(2) In a relational database, the same as a file; a collection of records.

table lookup Searching for data in a table, commonly used in data entry validation and any operation that must match an item of data with a known set of values.

tablet See *digitizer tablet*.

tabular form Same as *table view* with respect to printed output.

tabulate (1) To arrange data into a columnar format.

(2) To sum and print totals.

Tandem See *vendors*.

Tandy See *vendors*.

tape backup Use of magnetic tape for storing duplicate copies of hard disk files. QIC drives are the most widely used, but DAT and 8mm (Exabyte) formats are gaining ground.

tape drive Physical unit that holds, reads and writes the magnetic tape.

target computer Computer into which a program is loaded and run. Contrast with *source computer*.

target directory Directory into which data is being sent.

target disk Disk onto which data is recorded. Contrast with *source disk*.

target drive Drive containing the disk or tape onto which data is recorded. Contrast with *source drive*.

target language Language resulting from a translation process (assembler, compiler, etc.).

task switching Switching between active applications. See *context switching*.

TB, Tb See *terabyte* and *terabit*.

Tbit See *terabit*.

Tbits/sec (Tera**BITS** per **SEC**ond) Trillion bits per second.

TBps, Tbps (Tera**B**ytes **P**er **S**econd, Tera**B**its **P**er **S**econd) Trillion bytes per second. Trillion bits per second.

TByte See *terabyte*

Tbytes/sec (Tera**BYTES** per **SEC**ond) Trillion bytes per second.

T-carrier Digital transmission service from a common carrier. Introduced by AT&T in 1983 as a voice service, its use for data has grown steadily. T-carrier service is provided in 64Kbits/sec channels. Multiplexors are used at both ends to merge and split apart the signals. Capacities are: T1 (24 channels - 1.544Mbits/sec total capacity); T2 (96 channels - 6.312Mb); T3 requires optical fiber (672 channels - 45Mb).

TCP/IP (**T**ransmission **C**ontrol **P**rotocol/**I**nternet **P**rotocol) Communications protocols developed under contract from the Dept. of Defense (DOD) to internetwork dissimilar systems. It is a de facto UNIX standard, but is supported by operating systems from micro to mainframe. It is used by many corporations and almost all universities and federal agencies.

TDM (**T**ime **D**ivision **M**ultiplexing) Technique that interleaves (one after the other) several low-speed signals into one high-speed transmission. See *baseband*.

telecommunications Communicating information, including data, text, pictures, voice and video.

teleconferencing Conferencing between users via video, audio or computer.

Telenet Value-added, packet switching network that enables many varieties of terminals and computers to exchange data. It is a subsidiary of US Sprint.

teleprinter Typewriter-like terminal with a keyboard and built-in printer. Contrast with *video terminal*.

teletype mode Line-at-a-time output like a typewriter. Contrast with *full-screen*.

template (1) Plastic or stiff paper form that is placed over the function keys on a keyboard to identify their use.

(2) Programmatic and descriptive part of a programmable application; for example, a spreadsheet that contains only descriptions and formulas or a HyperCard stack that contains only programming and backgrounds. When the template is filled with data, it becomes a working application.

TELEPRINTER
TELEPRINTER

ter Third version.

tera Trillion. Abbreviated "T." It often refers to the precise value 1,099,511,627,776 since computer specifications are usually binary numbers. See *space/time*.

terabit One trillion bits. Also Tb, Tbit and T-bit. See *tera* and *space/time*.

terabyte One trillion bytes. Also TB, Tbyte and T-byte. See *tera* and *space/time*.

teraflops (**TERA F**Loating point **OP**erations per **S**econd) One trillion floating point operations per second.

terminal (1) I/O device for a computer that usually has a keyboard for input and a video screen or printer for output.

(2) Input device, such as a scanner, video camera or punched card reader.

(3) Output device in a network, such as a monitor, printer or card punch.

(4) Connector used to attach a wire.

terminal emulation Using a personal computer to simulate a mainframe or minicomputer terminal. See *virtual terminal*.

terminate and stay resident See TSR.

text Words, sentences and paragraphs. You're reading text. A page of text takes about 2,000 to 4,000 bytes in the computer. Software that works with text must be able to handle long, variable length strings in contrast with data processing, or database, systems that deal with pre-defined records made up of fields (quantity, amount due) fixed in position. Modern software handles text and data. See *memo field*.

text editor Software used to create and edit files that contain only text (batch files, address lists, source language programs, etc.). Unlike a word processor, it usually does not provide word wrap or formatting features such as underline, boldface or font changes. Editors designed for programming may provide automatic indention and multiple windows.

text file File that contains only text characters. Contrast with *graphics file* and *binary file*.

text mode Screen mode that displays only text. Contrast with *graphics mode*.

thermal printer Low-cost, low- to medium-resolution non-impact printer that uses heat-sensitive paper. Where the heated pins of the print head touch the paper, the paper darkens.

third-generation computer Computer that uses integrated circuits, disk storage and online terminals. The third generation started roughly in 1964 with the IBM System/360.

third-generation language Traditional high-level programming language such as FORTRAN, COBOL, BASIC, Pascal and C.

throughput Speed with which a computer processes data. It is a combination of internal processing speed, peripheral speeds (I/O) and the efficiency of the operating system and other system software all working together.

THz (**T**era**H**ert**Z**) One trillion cycles per second.

TI See *vendors*.

TIFF (**T**agged **I**mage **F**ile **F**ormat) Widely-used raster graphics file format developed by Aldus and Microsoft that handles monochrome, gray scale, 8-and 24-bit color.

tightly coupled Refers to two or more computers linked together and dependent on each other. One computer may control the other, or both computers may monitor each other. For example, a database machine is tightly coupled to the main processor. Two computers tied together for multiprocessing are tightly coupled. Contrast with *loosely coupled*, such as personal computers in a LAN.

tiled Display of objects side by side; for example, tiled windows cannot be overlapped on top of each other.

time slice Fixed interval of time allotted to each user or program in a multitasking or timesharing system.

timesharing Multiuser computer environment that lets users initiate their own sessions and access selected databases as required, such as when using online services. A system that serves many users, but for only one application, is technically not timesharing.

token passing Communications network access method that uses a continuously repeating frame (the token) that is transmitted onto the network by the controlling computer. When a terminal or computer wants to send a message, it waits for an empty token. When it finds one, it fills it with the address of the destination station and some or all of its message.

Token Ring Network IBM local area network that conforms to the IEEE 802.5 standard. All stations connect to a central wiring hub (star topology) through special twisted wire cable. The central hub makes it easier to troubleshoot failed units. It uses the token passing access method at 4 or 16Mbits/sec and passes tokens to up to 255 nodes in a ring-like sequence.

tool palette Collection of on-screen functions, typically graphics related, that are grouped in a menu structure for interactive selection.

toolkit Set of software routines that allow a program to be written for and work in a particular environment. The routines are called by the application program to perform various functions, for example, to display a menu or draw a graphic element.

topology In a communications network, the pattern of interconnection between nodes; for example, a bus, ring or star configuration.

touch screen Touch-sensitive display screen that uses a clear panel over the screen surface. The panel is a matrix of cells that transmits information indicating which cells are being pressed.

TP monitor (**T**ele**P**rocessing monitor or **T**ransaction **P**rocessing monitor) Communications control program that manages the transfer of data between multiple local and remote terminals and the application programs that serve them. CICS is an example in the IBM mainframe world. Tuxedo is an example for UNIX.

tpi (**T**racks **P**er **In**ch) Used to measure the density of tracks recorded on a disk or drum.

TPS (1) (**T**ransactions **P**er **S**econd) Number of transactions processed within one second.

(2) (**T**ransaction **P**rocessing **S**ystem) Originally used as an acronym for such a system, it now refers to the measurement of the system (#1 above).

track Storage channel on disk or tape. On disks, tracks are concentric circles (hard and floppy disks) or spirals (CDs and videodiscs). On tapes, they are parallel lines.

trackball Input device used in video games and as a mouse alternative. It is a stationary unit that contains a movable ball rotated with the fingers or palm and, correspondingly, moves the cursor on screen.

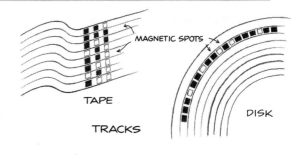

TAPE

TRACKS

MAGNETIC SPOTS

DISK

tractor feed Mechanism that provides fast movement of paper forms through a printer. It contains pins on tractors that engage the paper through perforated holes in its left and right borders.

transaction Activity or request. Orders, purchases, changes, additions and deletions are typical transactions stored in the computer. Queries and other requests are also transactions, but are usually just acted upon and not saved. Transaction volume is a major factor in figuring computer system size and speed.

PAYROLL	Employee Number	Today's Date	Hours Worked						
ORDER	Customer Number	Today's Date	Quantity	Product Number					
PAYMENT	Customer Number	Today's Date	Invoice Number	Amount Paid	Check Number				
PURCHASE	Purchase Order Number	Today's Date	Dept.	Authorized Agent	Vendor Number	Quantity	Product Number	Due Date
RECEIPT	Purchase Order Number	Today's Date	Quantity	Product Number					

TYPICAL DAILY OPERATIONS TRANSACTIONS

transaction file Collection of transaction records. The data in transaction files is used to update the data in master files, which contain the subjects of the organization. Transaction files also serve as audit trails and are usually transferred from online disks to the data library after some period of time. See *information system*.

PAY RAISE	Employee Number	Today's Date	Transaction Type	New rate	Management Authorization
CREDIT LIMIT CHANGE	Customer Number	Today's Date	New limit	Management Authorization	
PRODUCT DESCRIPTION CHANGE	Product Number	Today's Date	New Description	Management Authorization	

TYPICAL PERIODIC MAINTENANCE TRANSACTIONS

transaction processing Processing transactions as they are received by the computer. Also called *online* or *realtime* systems, master files are updated as soon as transactions are entered at terminals or arrive over communications lines. Contrast with *batch processing*.

transceiver Transmitter and receiver of analog or digital signals that comes in many forms; for example, a communications satellite transponder or a network adapter.

transfer rate Also called data rate, the transmission speed of a communications or computer channel. Transfer rates are measured in bits or bytes per second.

transistor Semiconductor device used to amplify a signal or open and close a circuit. In digital computers, it functions as an electronic switch.

transmit To send data over a communications line.

transmitter Device that generates signals. Contrast with *receiver*.

transparent Refers to a change in hardware or software that, after installation, causes no noticeable change in operation.

transponder Receiver and transmitter in a communications satellite. It receives a transmitted microwave signal from earth (uplink), amplifies it and retransmits it to earth at a different frequency (downlink). There are several transponders on a satellite.

transport protocol Communications protocol responsible for establishing a connection and ensuring that all data has arrived safely. It is defined in layer 4 of the OSI model.

triple twist Supertwist variation that twists crystals to 260 degrees for improved clarity.

true color (1) Ability to generate 16,777,216 colors (24-bit color). See *high color*.

(2) Ability to generate photo-realistic color images (greater than 24-bit color).

TrueType Scalable font technology from Apple that renders printer and screen fonts, used in Windows 3.1 and Mac System 7. Each TrueType font contains its own algorithms for converting the outline into bitmaps, unlike PostScript in which the algorithms are maintained in the rasterizing engine.

TSR (**T**erminate and **S**tay **R**esident) Refers to programs that remain in memory so that they can be instantly popped up over some other application by pressing a hotkey. The program is displayed either as a small window on top of the existing text or image, or it takes up the full screen. When the program is exited, the previous screen contents are restored.

TTL (**T**ransistor **T**ransistor **L**ogic) Digital circuit in which the output is derived from two transistors. Although TTL is a specific design method, it often refers generically to digital connections in contrast with analog connections.

turnaround document Paper document or punched card prepared for re-entry into the computer system. Paper documents are printed with OCR fonts for scanning Invoices and inventory stock cards are examples.

turnkey system Complete system of hardware and software delivered to the customer ready-to-run.

twisted pair Thin-diameter (22 to 26 gauge) insulated wires used in telephone wiring. The wires are twisted around each other to minimize interference from other pairs in the cable. Also UTP (unshielded twisted pair).

Tymnet (BTC Tymnet) Value-added, packet switching network that enables many varieties of terminals and computers to exchange data. Subsidiary of British Telecom.

Type 1 font See *PostScript*.

typeface Design of a set of printed characters, such as Helvetica and Times Roman. A typeface family includes the normal, bold, italic and bold-italic variations of the design.

typesetter See *phototypesetter*.

UMA (**U**pper **M**emory **A**rea) PC memory between 640K and 1024K.

UMB (**U**pper **M**emory **B**lock) Unused blocks in the UMA (640K-1M). A UMB provider is software that can load drivers and TSRs into this area.

unbundled Separate prices for each component in a system. Contrast with *bundled*.

undelete To restore the last delete operation that has taken place.

undo To restore the last editing operation that has taken place.

Unisys See *vendors*.

UNIVAC I (**UNIV**ersal **A**utomatic **C**omputer) First commercially-successful computer, introduced in 1951 by Remington Rand. Over 40 systems were sold. In 1952, it predicted Eisenhower's victory over Stevenson, and UNIVAC became synonymous with computer (for a while).

UNIX Multiuser, multitasking operating system from AT&T that runs on computers from micro to mainframe. UNIX is written in C (also developed at AT&T), which can be compiled into many different machine languages, causing UNIX to run in a wider variety of hardware than any other control program. UNIX has thus become synonymous with "open systems."

UNIVAC I
(Courtesty Unisys Corporation)

With the de facto standards that have been added over time, UNIX has evolved into the archetype environment for distributed processing and interoperability. TCP/IP communications protocols are used in the Internet, the world's largest series of interconnected networks. SMTP (Simple Mail Transfer Protocol) provides e-mail, Sun's NFS allows files to be distributed across the network, and its NIS provides a "Yellow Pages" directory. MIT's Kerberos provides network security, and its X Window sysem allows a user to run applications on other machines in the network simultaneously.

UnixWare Operating system for PCs from Univel, Inc. (joint venture of Novell and USL) based on UNIX System V Release 4.2. The single user version provides access to NetWare and runs UNIX, DOS and Windows applications. DR DOS is also included.

unload To remove a program from memory or take a tape or disk out of its drive.

unzip To decompress a file with the popular PKUNZIP shareware compression program.

UPC (**U**niversal **P**roduct **C**ode) Standard bar code printed on retail merchandise. It contains the vendor's identification number and the product number, which is read by passing the bar code over a scanner.

update To change data in a file or database. The terms update and edit are used synonymously.

upload See *download*.

UPS (**U**ninterruptible **P**ower **S**upply) Backup power for a computer system when the electrical power fails or drops to an unacceptable voltage level.

upward compatible Also called forward compatible. Refers to hardware or software that is compatible with succeeding versions. Contrast with *downward compatible*.

USENET (**USE**r **NET**work) Public access network on the Internet that provides user news and e-mail. It is a giant, dispersed bulletin board that is maintained by volunteers willing to provide news and mail feeds to other nodes.

user Any individual who interacts with the computer at an application level.

user friendly System that is easy to learn and easy to use.

user group Organization of users of a particular hardware or software product. Members share experiences and ideas to improve their understanding and use of a particular product.

user interface Combination of menus, screen design, keyboard commands, command language and help screens, which create the way a user interacts with a computer.

USL (**U**NIX **S**ystem **L**aboratories, Inc.) AT&T subsidiary formed in 1990, responsible for developing and marketing UNIX.

utility program Program that supports using the computer. Utility programs, or "utilities," provide file management capabilities, such as sorting, copying, comparing, listing and searching, as well as diagnostic and measurement routines that check the health and performance of the system.

UTP See *twisted pair*.

V.22bis CCITT standard (1984) for asynchronous and synchronous 2400 bps full-duplex modems for use on dial-up lines and two-wire leased lines, with fallback to V.22 1200 bps operation. It uses QAM modulation.

V.32 CCITT standard (1984) for asynchronous and synchronous 4800 and 9600 bps full-duplex modems using TCM modulation over dial-up or two-wire leased lines. TCM encoding may be optionally added. V.32 uses echo cancellation to achieve full-duplex transmission.

V.32bis CCITT standard (1991) for asynchronous and synchronous 4800, 7200, 9600, 12000 and 14400 bps full-duplex modems using TCM and echo cancellation. Supports rate renegotiation, which allows modems to change speeds as required.

V.42 CCITT standard (1989) for modem error checking that uses LAP-M as the primary protocol and provides MNP Classes 2 through 4 as an alternative protocol for compatibility.

V.42bis CCITT standard (1989) for modem data compression. It uses the British Telecom Lempel Ziv technique to achieve up to a 4:1 ratio. V.42bis implies the V.42 error checking protocol.

validity checking Routines in a data entry program that tests the input for correct and reasonable conditions, such as numbers falling within a range and correct spelling, if possible. See *check digit*.

value (1) Content of a field or variable. It can refer to alphabetic as well as numeric data. For example, in the expression, `state = "PA"`, PA is a value.

(2) In spreadsheets, the numeric data within the cell.

value-added network Communications network that provides services beyond normal transmission, such as automatic error detection and correction, protocol conversion and message storing and forwarding. Telenet and Tymnet are examples of value-added networks.

vaporware Software that has been advertised but not delivered.

VAR (**V**alue **A**dded **R**eseller) Organization that adds value to a system and resells it. For example, it could purchase a CPU and peripherals from different vendors and graphics software from another vendor and package it together as a specialized CAD system. See *OEM*.

variable In programming, a structure that holds data and is uniquely named by the programmer. It holds the data assigned to it until a new value is assigned or the program is finished.

variable length field Record structure that holds fields of varying lengths. For example, PAT SMITH takes nine bytes and GEORGINA WILSON BARTHOLOMEW takes 27. A couple of bytes of control information would also be added. If fixed length fields were used in this example, 27 or more bytes would have to be reserved for every name.

VAX (**V**irtual **A**ddress e**X**tension) Family of 32-bit computers from Digital Equipment Corporation introduced in 1977 with the VAX-11/780 model. VAXes range from desktop personal computers to large-scale mainframes all running the same VMS operating system.

vector In computer graphics, a line designated by its end points (x-y or x-y-z coordinates). When a circle is drawn, it is made up of many small vectors.

vector font Scalable font made of vectors (point-to-point line segments). It is easily scaled as are all vector-based images, but lacks the hints and mathematically-defined curves of outline fonts, such as Adobe Type 1 and TrueType.

vector graphics In computer graphics, a technique for representing a picture as points, lines and other geometric entities. Contrast with *raster graphics*.

vector processor Computer with built-in instructions that perform multiple calculations on vectors (one-dimensional arrays) simultaneously.

vendors The following hardware, software, consulting and service vendors represent all the majors and some of the more widely known.

ACER AMERICA CORP., PCs (Acer, Acros brands). San Jose, CA, 800/SEE-ACER.

ADOBE SYSTEMS, INC., PostScript language, fonts. Mtn. View, CA, 800/833-6687.

(ALR) ADVANCED LOGIC RESEARCH, PCs. Pioneered upgradable CPUs. Irvine, CA, 800/257-1230.

(AMD) ADVANCED MICRO DEVICES, Intel-compatible CPU chips. Sunnyvale, CA, 800/2929-AMD

ALDUS CORP., PageMaker, first desktop publishing. Seattle, WA, 800/332-5387.

AMDAHL CORP., First successful IBM-compatible mainframe manufacturer. Sunnyvale, CA, 800/538-8460.

(AMI) AMERICAN MEGATRENDS, INC., PC motherboards, ROM BIOS. Norcross, GA, 800/828-9264.

APPLE COMPUTER, Macintosh series, Apple IIe. Largest non-PC personal computer manufacturer. Pioneered microcomputers. Cupertino, CA, 800/776-2333.

ARTISOFT, INC., LANtastic peer-to-peer network. Tucson, AZ, 800/TINYRAM.

AST RESEARCH, INC., PCs, laptops. Irvine, CA, 714/727-4141.

ATARI, INC., ST and Falcon personal computers and video games. Founded 1972 by Nolan Bushnell. Sunnyvale, CA, 408/745-2000.

AUTODESK, INC., AutoCAD CAD software. Sausalito, CA, 800/964-6432.

(BBN) BOLT, BARANEK & NEWMAN, Consulting, software, research. At the forefront of major projects. Cambridge, MA, 800/422-2359.

BORLAND INT'L., INC., Programming languages (Turbo C, Turbo Pascal), dBASE, Paradox, Quattro Pro, Sidekick. Scotts Valley, CA, 800/331-0877.

BULL HN, Mini/mainframe manufacturer originally Honeywell's computer division, later merged with Groupe Bull of France and NEC of Japan. Billerica, MA, 800/999-2181.

CLARIS CORP., Software subsidiary of Apple Computer. MacDraw, MacWrite, FileMaker Pro, HyperCard, etc. Santa Clara, CA, 800/325-2747.

COMMODORE BUSINESS MACHINES, INC., Amiga personal computers. Introduced the PET personal computer in 1977. West Chester, PA, 800/66-AMIGA.

COMPAQ COMPUTER CORP., Known for rugged PCs. First successful clone. Reached $111 million sales in its first year. Houston, TX, 800/345-1518.

COMPUTER ASSOCIATES INT'L., INC., Software, micro to mainframe. Founded in 1976 by Charles Wang. Islindia, NY, 800/CALL-CAI.

CONNER PERIPHERALS, INC., Disk drives. San Jose, CA, 408/456-4500.

CONTROL DATA SYSTEMS, INC., Workstations, supercomputers. One of the first computer companies (1957) under Bill Norris. Minneapolis, MN, 612/893-4120.

CRAY RESEARCH, INC., Supercomputers originally designed by Seymour Cray, leading architect at Control Data. Egan, MN, 800/284-2729.

D&B SOFTWARE, 1990 merger of MSA and McCormack & Dodge software companies. Under leadership of John Imlay, CEO of MSA. Atlanta, GA, 800/234-3867.

DATA GENERAL CORP., Minicomputer pioneer. Founded 1968 by Edson De Castro. Westboro, MA, 800/328-2436.

DELL COMPUTER CORP., Mail-order PCs. Originally "PCs Limited" brand. Legitimized mail-order PCs with quality telephone support. Austin, TX, 800/289-3355.

(DEC) DIGITAL EQUIPMENT CORP., Pioneered minicomputers (1957) under Ken Olsen who retired in 1992. Minis, PCs, mainframes. Maynard, MA, 800/344-4825.

DIGITAL RESEARCH, INC., CP/M operating system. Later DR DOS. Founded 1976 by Gary Kildall. Acquired by Novell in 1991. Monterey, CA, 800/274-4DRI.

(EDS) ELECTRONIC DATA SYSTEMS, Pioneered facilities management. Founded 1962 by Ross Perot. Acquired by GM. Maryland Heights, MO, 314/344-5900.

EVEREX SYSTEMS, INC., PCs, servers. Fremont, CA.

GATEWAY 2000, Mail-order PCs. Pioneered lower PC prices in the early 1990s. N. Sioux City, SD, 800/523-2000

HAYES MICROCOMPUTER PRODUCTS, INC., Pioneered personal computer modem and modem language (Hayes AT command set). Atlanta, GA, 404/840-9200.

(HP) HEWLETT-PACKARD COMPANY, One of first minicomputer companies. Minis, workstations, PCs plus 10,000 electronic products. Founded 1939 by William Hewlett & David Packard. Palo Alto, CA, 800/752-0900.

HITACHI AMERICA, Monitors, CD ROM players, computers.

(IBM) INT'L. BUSINESS MACHINES CORP., World's largest computer co. Mainframes, minis, PCs. Founded 1911, named IBM in 1924 under T. J. Watson, Sr. Armonk, NY, 800/426-2468.

INTEL CORP., x86 CPU chips used in PCs. Santa Clara, CA, 800/538-3373.

LOTUS DEVELOPMENT CORP., First PC spreadsheet (1-2-3), Ami Pro, Lotus Notes, etc. Founded in 1981 by Mitch Kapor. Cambridge, MA, 800/343-5414.

MAXTOR CORP., Disk drives. San Jose, CA, 800/262-9867

MICRONICS COMPUTERS, INC., PC motherboards, electronics, laptops. Fremont, CA, 510/651-2300.

MICROSOFT CORP., DOS, Windows, programming languages, applications. Founded in 1975 by Bill Gates and Paul Allen. Redmond, WA, 800/227-4679.

MOTOROLA, INC., 68000 CPU chips (Macs, workstations). Schaumburg, IL.

NCR CORP., One of first computer companies. National Cash Register started in 1884 by John Patterson. Acquired by AT&T in 1991. Dayton, OH, 800/CALL-NCR.

NEC TECHNOLOGIES, INC., Pioneered multifrequency monitor with its MultiSync line. Boxborough, MA, 800/343-4418.

NORTHGATE COMPUTER SYSTEMS, INC., Mail-order PCs, Omnikey keyboards. Founded 1987. Minneapolis, MN, 800/548-1993.

NOVELL, INC., NetWare operating systems. Most widely-used networking software. Founded 1983 by Ray Noorda. Provo, UT, 800/453-1267.

(OSF) OPEN SOFTWARE FOUNDATION, UNIX-based open systems. Provides standards and products. Cambridge, MA, 617/621-8700.

ORACLE CORP., Oracle database system runs on more platforms than any other DBMS. Founded in 1977. Redwood Shores, CA, 800/ORACLE-1.

PACKARD BELL, INC., Complete line of PCs and peripherals. Founded in 1986. Chatsworth, CA, 818/886-4600.

PHOENIX TECHNOLOGIES, INC., PC ROM BIOS chips, electronics. Norwood, MA, 800/344-7200.

QUARTERDECK OFFICE SYSTEMS, DESQview environments, QEMM. Santa Monica, CA, 310/392-9851.

(SCO) THE SANTA CRUZ OPERATION, UNIX and XENIX operating systems. Santa Cruz, CA, 800/SCO-9694.

SEAGATE TECHNOLOGY, INC., Disk drives. Largest independent. Scotts Valley, CA, 800/468-3472.

SOFTWARE PUBLISHING CORP., Harvard Graphics, Superbase, etc. Santa Clara, CA, 800/447-7991.

SONY CORP. OF AMERICA, Monitors, CR ROM players, disk drives and diskettes. San Jose, CA, 800/352-7669.

SUN MICROSYSTEMS, INC., Largest supplier of UNIX-based systems (SPARC workstations). Founded in 1982 by Bill Joy. Mountain View, CA, 800/821-4643.

SYMANTEC CORP., Norton Utilities, etc. Cupertino, CA, 800/441-7234.

TANDEM COMPUTERS, INC., First fault-tolerant computers (1974) under Jim Treybig. Cupertino, CA, 800/538-3107.

TANDY CORP., PCs and electronics through Radio Shack chain acquired in 1963. TRS-80 was one of the first personal computers. Fort Worth, TX, 817/390-3011.

TEXAS INSTRUMENTS, INC., Chips, electronics, laptops. Founded 1930 as Geophysical Service, renamed TI in 1951. Dallas, TX, 800/527-3500.

TOSHIBA AMERICA INFO. SYSTEMS, INC., Pioneered laptop PCs. Irvine, CA, 800/334-3445.

UNISYS CORP., 1986 merger of Sperry and Burroughs, two of the oldest computer companies. Mainframes, minis, PCs. Blue Bell, PA, 800-448-1424.

(USL) UNIX SYSTEMS LABORATORIES, INC., AT&T subsidiary that develops and markets UNIX System V. Summit, NJ, 800/828-8649.

WANG LABORATORIES, INC., Early minicomputer company. WP leader in the 1970s. Founded 1951 by Dr. An Wang. Lowell, MA, 800/835-9264.

WESTERN DIGITAL CORP., Disk drives, controllers. "Paradise" display boards. Irvine, CA, 800/832-4778.

WORDPERFECT CORP., Most widely-used word processing software. Founded 1979. Orem, UT, 800/321-5906.

WORDSTAR INT'L., INC., WordStar was the first full-featured word processor for personal computers. Founded 1978. Novato, CA, 800/227-5609.

XEROX CORP., Pioneered graphical interface on Alto computer at PARC Research Center. Introduced concept on Star workstation 1981. Palo Alto, CA, 800/626-6775.

ZENITH DATA SYSTEMS CORP., PCs, monitors. Pioneered laptops. Buffalo Grove, IL, 800/227-3360.

Ventura Publisher Desktop publishing program for PCs and the Macintosh from Ventura Software, Inc. (a Xerox company), that provides full-scale pagination for large documents.

version number Identification of a release of software. The difference between Version 2.2 and 2.3 can be night and day, since new releases not only add features, but often correct annoying bugs. What's been driving you crazy may have been fixed!

vertical scan frequency Number of times an entire display screen is refreshed, or redrawn, per second. For example, VGA in the U.S. is generally 56 to 60Hz; in Europe, 70Hz and above. Contrast with *horizontal scan frequency*.

VESA See *standards bodies*.

VGA (**V**ideo **G**raphics **A**rray) IBM video display standard built into most PS/1 and PS/2 models that provides medium-resolution text and graphics. It has become the minimum standard for all PCs. VGA supports previous CGA and EGA modes and requires an analog monitor. Its highest-resolution mode is 640x480 with 16 colors, but VESA and third parties have boosted colors and resolutions to 800x640 and 1024x768 (Super VGA).

VGA pass through Feature of a high-resolution display adapter that couples internally with a VGA display adapter and passes its signals through to the monitor.

video display board Expansion board that plugs into a personal computer and generates the text and graphics images for the monitor's screen. Also called a *display adapter, graphics adapter, graphics card, video adapter, video card* or *video controller*, it determines the resolution and number of colors on screen.

video RAM Specially-designed memory circuits on a video display board that are used to hold the image that appears on the video screen.

video terminal Data entry device that uses a keyboard for input and a display screen for output. Although the display screen resembles a TV, it usually does not accept TV/video signals.

Virtual 8086 Mode Subset of Protected Mode that runs tasks as if each one were running in an invidual 8086 CPU.

virtual desktop Desktop beyond the borders of the viewing screen. Rather than overlapping windows or reducing them to an icon, a virtual desktop simulates a giant desktop that lets you browse several full-size documents using a virtual screen or other navigation method.

virtual machine (1) Computer that runs multiple operating systems with each operating system running its own programs; for example, an IBM mainframe running under VM or a 386 PC running multiple DOS applications in its virtual mode.

(2) Virtual memory computer.

virtual memory Technique that simulates more memory than actually exists by breaking up the program into segments, called *pages*, and bringing in as many pages as possible at one time. The rest of the pages remain on disk until required.

virtual reality Artificial reality that projects the user into a 3-D space generated by computer. Implementations by AutoDesk and others include the use of a data glove and head-mounted stereoscopic display, which allow users to point to and manipulate illusory objects in their view. See *cyberspace*.

virtual screen Screen area beyond the borders of the viewing screen. The viewing screen serves as a scrollable window that navigates around the larger screen. Video display boards may offer this capability; for example, you could browse a 1280x1024 viewing area with an 800x600 screen resolution. See *virtual desktop*.

virtual storage Same as *virtual memory*.

virtual terminal Terminal emulation that allows access to a foreign system. Often refers to a personal computer gaining access to a mini or mainframe.

virtual toolkit Development software that creates programs for several computer environments. Its output may require additional conversions or translations to produce executable programs.

virtualize (1) To activate a program in virtual memory.

(2) To create a virtual screen.

virus Software used to destroy data in a computer. After the virus code is written, it is buried within an existing program. Once that program is executed, the virus code is activated and attaches copies of itself to other programs in the system. Infected programs copy the virus to other programs. See *worm*.

VisiCalc First electronic spreadsheet. It was introduced in 1978 for the Apple II. It launched an industry and was almost entirely responsible for the Apple II being used in business. Thousands of $3,000 Apples were bought to run the $150 VisiCalc.

visual programming Developing programs with tools that allow menus, buttons and other graphics elements to be selected from a palette and drawn and built on screen. It may include developing source code by visually interacting with flow charts that graphically display the logic paths and associated code.

VL-bus (**V**ESA **L**ocal-**BUS**) PC local bus endorsed by VESA that provides a 32-bit data path at speeds up to 40MHz (up to 66MHz for controllers built on the motherboard). The VL-bus slot uses a 32-bit Micro Channel connector adjacent to the standard ISA, EISA or Micro Channel slot, allowing vendors to design boards that use only the local bus or both buses at the same time. VL-bus supports up to three peripherals as well as bus mastering. See *local bus*.

VM (**V**irtual **M**achine) IBM mainframe operating system, originally developed by its customers and eventually adopted as a system product (VM/SP). It can run multiple operating systems within the computer at the same time, each one running its own programs. CMS (Conversational Monitor System) provides interactive capability.

VMS (1) (**V**irtual **M**emory **S**ystem) Operating system used in Digital's VAX series. VMS applications will run on any VAX from the MicroVAX to the largest VAX.

(2) (**V**oice **M**essaging **S**ystem) See *voice mail*.

voice mail Computerized telephone answering system that digitizes incoming voice messages and stores them on disk. It usually provides auto attendant capability, which uses prerecorded messages to route the caller to the appropriate person, department or mail box.

voice messaging Using voice mail as an alternative to electronic mail, in which voice messages are intentionally recorded, not because the recipient was not available.

voice processing Computerized handling of voice, which includes voice store and forward, voice response, voice recognition and text to speech technologies.

voice recognition Conversion of spoken words into computer text. Speech is first digitized and then matched against a dictionary of coded waveforms. The matches are converted into text as if the words were typed on the keyboard.

voice response Generation of voice output by computer. It provides pre-recorded information either with or without selection by the caller. Interactive voice response allows interactive manipulation of a database.

volume (1) Physical storage unit, such as a hard disk, floppy disk, disk cartridge or reel of tape.

(2) Logical storage unit that spans some number of physical drives.

volume label (1) Name assigned to a disk (usually optional).

(2) Identifying stick-on label attached to the outside of a tape reel or disk cartridge.

von Neumann architecture Sequential nature of computers: an instruction is analyzed, data is processed, the next instruction is analyzed, and so on. Hungarian-born John von Neumann (1903-1957), an internationally renowned mathematician, promoted the stored program concept in the 1940s.

VRAM See *video RAM*.

VSE (**D**isk **O**perating **S**ystem/**V**irtual **S**torage **E**xtended) IBM multiuser, multitasking operating system that typically runs on IBM's 43xx series. It used to be called DOS, but due to the abundance of DOS PCs, it is now referred to as VSE.

VT 100, 200... (**V**ideo **T**erminal) Series of asynchronous display terminals from Digital that are used on its PDP and VAX computers. They are available in text and graphics models in both monochrome and color.

VTAM (**V**irtual **T**elecommunications **A**ccess **M**ethod) Also called ACF/VTAM (Advanced Communications Function/VTAM), software that controls communications in an IBM SNA environment. It supports a wide variety of network protocols, including SDLC and Token Ring. VTAM can be thought of as the network operating system of SNA.

wafer Base material in chip making. It is a slice, approx. 1/30" thick, from a salami-like silicon crystal from 3 to 6" in diameter. The wafer goes through a series of photomasking, etching and implantation steps.

wafer scale integration Next evolution in semiconductor technology. It builds a gigantic circuit on an entire wafer. Just as the integrated circuit eliminated cutting apart thousands of transistors from the wafer only to wire them back again on circuit boards, wafer scale integration eliminates cutting apart the chips.

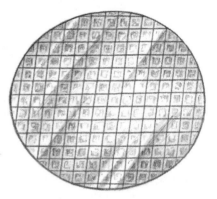

SILICON WAFER

wait state Amount of time spent waiting for some operation to take place. It can refer to a variable length of time a program has to wait before it can be processed, or it may refer to a specific duration of time, such as a machine cycle.

When memory is too slow to respond to the CPU's request for it, wait states are introduced until the memory can catch up.

WAN (**W**ide **A**rea **N**etwork) Communications network that covers wide geographic areas, such as states and countries. See *MAN* and *LAN*.

wand Hand-held optical reader used to read typewritten fonts, printed fonts, OCR fonts and bar codes. The wand is waved over each line of characters or codes in a single pass.

Wang See *vendors*.

warm boot Restarting the computer by performing a reset operation (pressing reset, Ctrl-Alt-Del, etc.). See *cold boot* and *boot*.

warm start Same as *warm boot*.

wavelength Distance between crests of a wave, computed by speed divided by frequency.

Weitek coprocessor High-performance math coprocessor for micro and minicomputers from Weitek Corp. Since 1981, the company has been making coprocessors for CAD and graphics workstations. In order to use a Weitek coprocessor, software must be written for it.

Whetstones Benchmark program that test floating point operations. See *Dhrystones*.

WIN.INI (**WIN**dows **INI**tialization) File read by Windows on startup that contains data about the current environment (desktop, fonts, sounds, etc.) and individual applications. SYSTEM.INI, another startup file, contains data about the hardware (drivers, 386 Enhanced Mode settings, etc.).

window (1) Rectangular, scrollable viewing area. May refer to a scrollable list of entries or to a re-sizable window that contains the entire application.

(2) Reserved area of memory.

(3) Time period.

Windows Graphics-based operating environment from Microsoft that integrates with DOS. It provides a desktop environment similar to the Macintosh, in which each active application is displayed in a re-sizable, movable window on screen.

In order to use all the features of Windows, applications must be written specifically for it. However, Windows also runs DOS applications and can be used as the primary operating environment from which all programs are launched.

windows environment Any operating system, operating system extension or application program that provides multiple windows on screen. DESQview, Windows, PM, MultiFinder and X Window are examples.

Windows for Workgroups Version of Windows 3.1 that incorporates peer-to-peer networking and includes e-mail.

Windows Metafile Windows file format that holds vector graphics, bitmaps and text. Its vector format is becoming popular for graphics interchange.

Windows NT (Windows **N**ew **T**echnology) Advanced operating system from Microsoft for 386s and up, MIPS and Alpha CPUs, scheduled for 1993. It runs applications written for DOS, Windows 3.x and NT. NT does not use DOS, it is a self-contained operating system.

windows program (1) Software that adds a windows capability to an existing operating system.

(2) (Windows program) Application program written to run under Microsoft Windows.

Winjet Hardware/software from LaserMaster, Eden Prarie, MN, that turns LaserJets into high-resolution PostScript printers. It provides up to 1200 dpi on the LaserJet 4. One board fits in the PC, a second board is inserted into the LaserJet.

Winmark Measurement of Windows graphics performance as a weighted average of 12 Winbench graphics benchmarks. Common VGA adapters are rated around two million Winmarks. Fast graphics accelerators can achieve 20 million and more.

wizzy wig See *WYSIWYG*.

word (1) Computer's internal storage unit. Refers to the amount of data it can hold in its registers. For example, at the same clock rate, a 16-bit computer processes two bytes in the same time it takes an 8-bit computer to process one byte.

(2) Primary text element, identified by a word separator (blank space, comma, etc.) before and after a group of contiguous characters.

Word for Windows See *Microsoft Word.*

word processing Creation and management of text documents by computer. Except for labels and envelopes, it has replaced the electric typewriter in most offices, because of the ease in which documents can be edited, searched and reprinted. Advanced word processors function as elementary desktop publishing systems and support graphics as well as an infinite variety of fonts.

word processor (1) Software that provides word processing functions on a computer.

(2) Computer specialized for word processing functions.

word wrap Feature of word processing and text handling systems that aligns text automatically within preset margins. Words "wrap around" to the next line automatically.

WordPerfect Full-featured word processing program from WordPerfect Corp., Orem, UT. Introduced in 1980, it runs on most all personal computers and some workstations, and is the most widely used word processor in the world.

WordStar Full-featured PC word processing program from WordStar Int'l., Novato, CA. Introduced in 1978 for CP/M machines, it was the first program to give sophisticated word processing capabilities to personal computer users at far less cost than the dedicated word processors of the time. WordStar keyboard commands have become de facto standards.

workgroup Two or more individuals who share files and databases. LANs designed around workgroups provide electronic sharing of required data.

working directory See *current directory.*

worksheet Same as *spreadsheet.*

workstation (1) High-performance, single-user microcomputer or minicomputer that has been specialized for graphics, CAD, CAE or scientific applications.

(2) Personal computer in a network. Contrast with *server* and *host.* See *client.*

(3) Any terminal or personal computer.

worm (1) Destructive program that replicates itself throughout disk and memory, using up the computers resources and eventually putting the system down. See *virus* and *logic bomb.*

(2) Program that moves throughout a network and deposits information at each node for diagnostic purposes, or causes idle computers to share some of the processing workload.

(3) (WORM) (**W**rite **O**nce **R**ead **M**any) Storage device that uses an optical medium that can be recorded only once. Updating requires destroying the existing data (all 0s made 1s), and writing the revised data to an unused part of the disk.

wrist rest Platform used to raise the wrist to keyboard level for typing.

wrist support Product that prevents and provides a therapy for carpal tunnel syndrome by keeping the hands in a neutral wrist position.

write To store data in memory or record onto a storage medium, such as disk or tape. Read and write is analogous to play and record on an audio tape recorder.

write error Inability to store into memory or record onto disk or tape. Malfunctioning memory cells or damaged portions of the disk or tape's surface will cause those areas to be unusable.

write only code Jokingly refers to source code that is difficult to understand.

write protect Prohibits erasing or editing a disk file. See *file protection*.

write protect notch Small, square cutout on the side of a floppy disk used to prevent it from being written and erased. On 5.25" floppies, the notch must be covered for protection. To protect a 3.5" diskette, press the slide lever toward the edge of the disk uncovering a hole (upper left side viewed from the back).

The two common formats use exact opposite methods!

WYSIWYG (**W**hat **Y**ou **S**ee **I**s **W**hat **Y**ou **G**et) Pronounced "wizzy-wig." Refers to text and graphics appearing on screen the same as they print. To have WYSIWYG text, a screen font must be installed that matches each printer font. Otherwise, a 24-point font may display in correct size relationship to a 10-point font, but it won't look like the printed typeface.

It is almost impossible to get 100% identical representation, because screen and printer resolutions rarely match. Even a 300 dpi printer has a higher resolution than almost every monitor.

WYSIWYG

X See X *Window*.

x86 Refers to the Intel 8086 CPU family (8086, 8088, 80286, 386, 486, Pentium). Starting with the 386, Intel dropped the "80" prefix in its manuals. Same as 80x86.

x86 SPECIFICATIONS

CPU # (Word size in bits)	CPU Speed (MHz)	BUS (Bits)	Max. RAM (Bytes)	FLOPPY DISK (Bytes)	Typical HARD DISK (MB)	OS
8088 (16)	4.8-9.5	8	1M	5.25" 360K	10-20	DOS
8086 (16)	6-12	16	1M	3.5" 720K 3.5" 1.44M	10-40	DR DOS
286 (16)	6-16	16	16M	5.25" 360K 5.25" 1.2M 3.5" 720K	20-80	DOS, DR DOS, OS/2 Ver. 1.x
386DX (32)	8	32	4G	3.5" 1.44M 3.5" 2.88M	60-200	DOS, DR DOS, OS/2 1.x OS/2 2.x UNIX Windows NT
386SX (32)	16-25	16	16M		40-100	
386SL (32)	20-25	16	16M		40-100	
486DX (32)	25-66	32	4G		100-1500	
486SX (32)	16-25	32	4G		60-150	
Pentium (586)	Due 1st Qtr. '93					

X.400 CCITT/ISO standard mail and messaging protocol.

X.500 CCITT/ISO standard protocol for maintaining online address directories for electronic mail.

Xbase dBASE-like language such as Clipper and FoxPro. dBASE created an industry of dBASE compilers and dBASE-compatible DBMSs. Proposals have been submitted to ANSI by major vendors to standardize the Xbase language.

XGA (**Ex**tended **G**raphics **A**rray) IBM high-resolution video display standard optimized for graphical user interfaces. Its highest resolution (XGA-2) is 1024x768 non-interlaced with 64K colors.

Xmodem First widely-used file transfer protocol for personal computer communications (developed by Ward Cristensen for CP/M machines). It has been superseded by Ymodem and Zmodem.

XMS (e**X**tended **M**emory **S**pecification) Programming standard that allows DOS applications to cooperatively use extended memory . It provides functions that reserve, release and transfer data to and from extended memory and the HMA.

XT (**Ex**tended **T**echnology) First IBM PC with a hard disk, introduced in 1983.

XT bus Refers to the 8-bit bus architecture used in the first PC. See *AT bus*.

XT class Refers to PCs that use the 8088/8086 CPU and the 8-bit bus.

XT interface See *XT bus*.

X Window Formally X *Window System*, also called X *Windows* and X, it is a windowing system developed at MIT, which runs under UNIX and all major operating systems. X lets users run applications on other computers in the network and view the output on their own screen. See *DESQview/X*.

XyWrite III Plus Pronounced "zy-write." PC word processing program from the XyQuest division of The Technology Group, Baltimore, MD. Used extensively by major magazines and newspapers, it is noted for its speed and flexibility.

Signature, successor to XyWrite III Plus, was developed by XyQuest, Inc. and IBM with built-in migration for XyWrite and IBM DisplayWrite files. XyWrite 4 is the successor to both Signature and XyWrite III Plus.

Ymodem File transfer protocol for personal computer communications. It is faster than Xmodem and transfers file name to the recipient before sending the data. See *Zmodem*.

Z80 8-bit microprocessor from Zilog Corp. that was the successor to the Intel 8080. The Z80 was widely used in first-generation personal computers that used the CP/M operating system.

zap Command that typically deletes the data within a file but leaves the file structure intact so that new data can be entered.

zip (1) To compress a file with the PKZIP file compression program.

(2) (ZIP) (**Z**ig-**Z**ag **I**nline **P**ackage) Similar to a DIP, but smaller and tilted on its side for mounting on boards with limited space.

ziwrite See *XyWrite III Plus*.

Zmodem Latest file transfer protocol that is very popular. It sends file name, date and size before sending the data. It responds well to changing line conditions and satellite transmission. In the event of a line failure, Zmodem can begin sending from where it stopped when the carrier dropped and ensure that the remote file is fully restored. This is great insurance when downloading extremely long files.

1-2-3 See *Lotus 1-2-3*.

10BaseT See *Ethernet*.

286 Successor to the 8088 CPU used in the first PC (XT-class). Refers to the Intel 80286 CPU chip or to a PC (AT-class) that uses it. It is more responsive than an XT and isn't limited to its infamous one-megabyte barrier. The 286 is a 16-bit multitasking microprocessor that can address 16MB of memory and 1GB of virtual memory. See *x86*.

32-bit processing In a PC, refers to programs written for the 386's native mode. All registers, pointers and addresses use the full 32 bits. Although the 386 is a 32-bit machine, under DOS, it runs applications in Real Mode, which functions as a 16-bit 8088, the CPU in the first PC.

360 See *System/360*.

370 See *System/370*.

386 Successor to the 286. Also known as the 386DX, it refers to the Intel 386 CPU chip or to a PC that uses it. The 386 is faster than the 286, addresses more memory, and allows both extended and expanded (EMS) memory to be allocated on demand. The 386 is a 32-bit multitasking CPU that is more responsive to Windows and graphics-intensive applications than the 16-bit 286. The 386SX runs at slower speeds, uses less power and runs cooler than the full 386, but takes twice as long to address memory (16-bit data bus instead of 32 bit). The 386SL chip is designed for laptops with built-in power management that lets it idle at lower speeds. Except for memory and video controller, the 386SL and one other chip make up almost the entire computer. See *x86*.

386MAX DOS memory manager for 386s and up from Qualitas, Inc., Bethesda, MD, noted for its advanced capabilities. BlueMAX is a version for PS/2 models.

386SLC IBM version of the 386SX that includes an internal 8KB memory cache. It includes power management capabilities and runs as fast as a 386DX.

387 Math coprocessor for the 386.

3270 Family of IBM mainframe terminals and related protocols (includes 3278 mono and 3279 color terminal). See *IRMAboard*.

486 Successor to the 386. Also known as the 486DX, it refers to the Intel 486 CPU chip or to a PC that uses it. It runs twice as fast as the 386 and provides the speed necessary for today's graphical interfaces. Its built-in math coprocessor is often required by CAD applications.

The "Speed Doubler" DX2 is a 486 with double the internal speed. For example, a 486/50DX2 accesses RAM and other chips on the motherboard at 25MHz but processes internally at 50MHz. DX chips may be replaced with Intel's OverDrive DX2 chip.

The 486SX runs at slower clock speeds and doesn't include the math coprocessor. 486SXs can also be upgraded to DX2s, which includes the coprocessor. The 486SL chip is designed for laptops. It includes built-in power management and uses 3.3 volts instead of the traditional five volts.

486/25, 486/33, etc. refer to the speed of the CPU. The second number is the clock speed: 486/25 means a 25MHz quartz crystal sets the timing for the machine.

486DLC 486SX-compatible CPU from Cyrix Corp. that is pin compatible with the 386DX. Designed for upgrading 386s, it comes in a variety of speeds including clock doubling versions.

486SLC (1) 486SX-compatible CPU from Cyrix Corporation that is pin compatible with the 386SX, has a 1K cache and uses a 16-bit bus. It provides an upgrade path for 386SXs.

(2) IBM version of the 486SX.

4GL See *fourth-generation language*.

586 See *Pentium*.

68000 Family of 32-bit microprocessors from Motorola that are the CPUs in Macintoshes and a variety of workstations. The 68000 addresses up to 16MB of memory and uses a 16-bit data bus. The 68020 addresses up to 4GB of memory and uses a 32-bit data bus. The 68030 runs at higher clock speeds and has a built-in memory cache. The 68040 is a redesigned version that runs up to three times as fast as a 68030.

7-track Refers to older magnetic tape formats that record 6-bit characters plus a parity bit.

8080 8-bit microprocessor from Intel introduced in 1974. It was the successor to the 8008 (first commercial 8-bit microprocessor) and precursor to the 8086 family.

8086 Introduced in 1978, the 16-bit CPU that defines the base architecture of Intel's x86 chip family (XT, AT, 386, 486, Pentium). 8086 CPUs were used in some XT-class machines. See *x86*.

8088 Intel 16-bit CPU chip used in first-generation PCs (XT class), which addresses only one megabyte of memory. It is a slower version (8-bit bus) of the 8086, originally chosen to ease conversion from
8-bit CP/M programs, the predominate business applications of the early 1980s. See *x86*.

80x86 See *x86*.

80286, 80386, 80486 See *286, 386* and *486*

8514/A IBM high-resolution display adapter that provides an interlaced display of 1024x768 pixels with up to 256 colors or 64 shades of gray. It contains a built-in coprocessor and is designed to coexist with VGA for dual monitor capability. Developed for Micro Channel machines, third-party vendors provide non-interlaced versions for AT-bus machines.

9-track Refers to magnetic tape that records 8-bit bytes plus parity, or nine parallel tracks. This is the common format for 1/2" tape reels.